Holy Ghost Fireworks

The Generational Workings of the Holy Spirit

Dr. Gbenga Mathew Owotoki

Copyright©2018 by Dr. G.M Owotoki

ISBN: 978-978-54253-1-4

ALL RIGHTS RESERVED TO THE AUTHOR...

PUBLISHED BY Hephzibah Network Publishing

Email: gmattoki@gmail.com

All scriptural quotations are taken from the various translations of the Bible and are indicated as such.

No Part of this book may be reproduced or transmitted in any form or by any means, graphics, electronic, or mechanical including recording, taping or by any information storage or retrieval system, without the written permission of the publisher.

For copyright information and other requests please contact the Author at the above email address.

Acknowledgement

I cannot but appreciate everyone that have played one role or the other as I continue in my journey of Purpose. I thank God for the womb that "housed" me. My mum has been a great inspiration. She nurtured me early in the path of righteousness. Thank you mum.

Thank God for everyone that have lifted my hands and supported me. The Hephzibah and Mountaintop family. God has used you as an anchor. I appreciate you all. Greater days are here. For those that have impacted on my life and ministry. You mean so much to me. The Lord bless you.

I want to say a big thank you to my jewel of inestimable value. You have been my rock and backbone. Love you plenty and to my boys Leslie and Lemuel, you give me so much joy and daddy loves you without bars.

Table Of contents

ACKNOWLEDGEMENT 3

INTRODUCTION 5

CHAPTER ONE : THE NEED FOR THE HOLY SPIRIT IN OUR GENERATION 10

CHAPTER TWO : WHEN THE HOLY SPIRIT SHOWS UP 28

CHAPTER 3 : THE STIRRING OF THE SPIRIT BEFORE THE ADVENT OF CHRIST.................. 41

CHAPTER 4 : MEN AND WOMEN WHO LIT UP THE IRON AGE 60

CHAPTER 5 : BLAZING SPIRITUAL "COMETS" WHO SHOOK THE MEDIEVAL TIMES.......... 81

CHAPTER 6 : THE GREAT AWAKENING OF MODERN ERA... 104

CHAPTER 7 : THESE SIGNS SHALL FOLLOW THOSE WHO BELIEVE 127

CONCLUSIONS: 153

OTHER BOOKS BY THE AUTHOR... 161

CONTACT DETAILS FOR THE AUTHOR: 161

Introduction

> THE EARTH WAS FORMLESS AND VOID, AND
> DARKNESS WAS OVER THE SURFACE OF THE
> DEEP, AND THE SPIRIT OF GOD WAS
> MOVING OVER THE SURFACE OF THE
> WATERS. GENESIS 1:2 (NASB)

The Holy Spirit was there in the very beginning of creation. Pharaoh acknowledged that the Holy Spirit was with Joseph to interpret the dreams and to wisely lead Egypt through plenty and famine. YHWH told Moses that Bezalel was filled with the Holy Spirit in wisdom, understanding, knowledge and skill in workmanship. The Holy Spirit came upon Balaam and he prophesied blessings upon Israel contrary to what Balak wanted when he hired the prophet to curse God's chosen people. Saul prophesied with the company of prophets when the Holy Spirit came upon him. The Holy Spirit came upon Azariah, son of Oded to give guidance to King Asa; the Holy Spirit came upon Zechariah, the son of Jehoiada to rebuke King Josiah.

Jesus of Nazareth was born of the virgin (as spoken by God as the Seed of the woman and prophesied by Isaiah as Immanuel) when Mary conceived through the power of the Holy Ghost. John was announced to be born filled with the Holy Ghost from his mother's womb. Mary's cousin Elizabeth with John in her womb was filled with the Holy Ghost and spoke to Mary of being blessed with God performing what He has foretold. Zechariah, Elizabeth's husband, prophesied of his son John. The Holy Ghost was upon the just and devout Simeon waiting for the Messiah to come. The Holy Ghost revealed to him that he would not die before he sees the Messiah. He took in his arms the eight-day-old Jesus when He was presented in the temple in Jerusalem. The Holy Ghost descended upon Jesus in the bodily form of a dove when He was baptized by John in the River Jordan. John spoke that Jesus would baptize with the Holy Ghost and fire.

Jesus was filled with the Holy Ghost and went into the wilderness to be tempted by the devil. He was victorious over all the temptations. He spoke of casting out evil spirits by the Holy Spirit. He warned of blasphemy against the Holy Ghost, a sin that cannot be forgiven. He assured His disciples that the Holy Spirit would remain with them forever. He would supply the utterance when they testify of Jesus. He commanded His disciples to remain in Jerusalem and await the Holy Spirit coming upon them. The Holy Ghost will come upon them with power!

The Holy Ghost filled the disciples gathered in the upper room in Jerusalem on the day of Pentecost. They all spoke in tongues!

This signaled the workings of the Holy Ghost through believers. Three thousand were saved on that day. Signs and wonders were done in the Name of Jesus. The lame walked, the blind see and the dead were raised. Peter's shadow healed many. Paul's handkerchiefs healed more. The Holy Spirit worked all these miraculous wonders. Stephen filled with the Holy Ghost shut down the arguments of the Hellenistic Jews. Phillip filled with the Holy Ghost showed signs and wonders beyond what Simon the Sorcerer could ever do; Peter and John came to Samaria, laid hands on believers and they received the baptism of the Holy Ghost. The Holy Spirit commanded Phillip to run alongside the Ethiopian eunuch's chariot, preached Jesus through the text in Isaiah the eunuch was reading, baptized him in water along the road. The Holy Spirit then caught away Phillip and he ended up in Azotus.

> GOD GAVE JESUS OF NAZARETH THE HOLY SPIRIT AND POWER. JESUS WENT ABOUT DOING GOOD DEEDS. HE HEALED ALL THOSE WHO WERE HELD BY THE DEVIL. GOD WAS WITH HIM.
> ACTS 10:38 (WE)

Peter preached Jesus to Cornelius and his household. The two met through visions from the Holy Spirit. On that day, while Peter was yet preaching, the Holy Ghost came upon all those listening in that household. The Holy Spirit that was with Jesus of Nazareth was now with every believer.

John would record what Jesus said regarding the Holy Spirit in the gospel he wrote. Paul would expound on the role of the Holy Spirit in his epistles to the Romans and Corinthians. Peter, John, Jude and the author of the book of Hebrews all mentioned the Holy Ghost and His workings.

This book will trace these workings of the Holy Spirit from one generation to the next. It will testify to the mighty works of the Holy Spirit from the Old Testament to the New, from the first century disciples to present-day believers, from ardent Christians of the past to those awaiting the outpouring promised in the last of the last days. It will clearly expound the work of the Holy Spirit Jesus first mentioned to the disciples in the Upper Room the night He was betrayed. It will speak of the great need of that same Holy Ghost in this present generation. It will succinctly point out the indomitable and unmistakable presence of the Holy Spirit. The same Holy Spirit in Creation is the same Holy Spirit in the Jordan River and is still the same Holy Spirit on the Day of Pentecost. The Holy Spirit is the same Greater One in every believer.

Jesus is the same yesterday, today and forever. The Holy Spirit is the same. After all, the Holy Spirit is God like the Father and the Son.

Chapter One
The Need for the Holy Spirit in our Generation

> BUT I TELL YOU THE TRUTH, IT IS TO YOUR ADVANTAGE THAT I GO AWAY; FOR IF I DO NOT GO AWAY, THE HELPER (COMFORTER, ADVOCATE, INTERCESSOR—COUNSELOR, STRENGTHENER, STANDBY) WILL NOT COME TO YOU; BUT IF I GO, I WILL SEND HIM (THE HOLY SPIRIT) TO YOU [TO BE IN CLOSE FELLOWSHIP WITH YOU]. AND HE, WHEN HE COMES, WILL CONVICT THE WORLD ABOUT [THE GUILT OF] SIN [AND THE NEED FOR A SAVIOR], AND ABOUT RIGHTEOUSNESS, AND ABOUT JUDGMENT: ABOUT SIN [AND THE TRUE NATURE OF IT], BECAUSE THEY DO NOT BELIEVE IN ME [AND MY MESSAGE]; ABOUT RIGHTEOUSNESS [PERSONAL INTEGRITY AND GODLY CHARACTER], BECAUSE I AM GOING TO MY FATHER AND YOU WILL NO LONGER SEE ME; ABOUT JUDGMENT [THE CERTAINTY OF IT], BECAUSE THE RULER OF THIS WORLD (SATAN) HAS BEEN JUDGED AND CONDEMNED.
>
> JOHN 16:7-11 (AMP)

Jesus made it very clear. Christianity has muddied the waters, so to speak. The Greek word used was *Paracletos* literally One called alongside to help. This was the perfect description of the Holy Ghost to be given to the disciples first and to all believers afterwards. The disciples saw the life of God in Jesus (John would testify to this in his first epistle) and was promised they would have the same. The disciples adhered to these words faithfully. They did not take anything upon themselves; they took Jesus' words literally and became fully dependent on the Holy Spirit.

It was not about crusades, concerts, film showings, and athletic events. It was the Holy Ghost! It was not tract distribution, door-to-door and friendship evangelism. It was the Holy Ghost! It was not programs, pass-it-on seminars, and evangelism explosions. It was the Holy Ghost!

It is still the Holy Ghost! Only the Holy Ghost can convict a sinner of his sinfulness and great, great, great need of a Savior. Only the Holy Ghost can show the world the great wickedness prevailing in every part of the earth and make the invitation to return to God. The Holy Ghost as the Divine Author of the Sacred Scriptures has already spoken of this in the book of beginnings – Genesis.

After creating everything to serve God and man, the Holy Spirit ends the very first chapter of the narrative with the description 'very good' after a series of exclamatory 'good' on each day of creation. The adjectives were applied to all creation and specifically to the crowning glory of creation – man on the sixth day. The next narrative was not good.

Woman (with man!) failed to be faithful to God's word and reaped death in the process. Sin entered. Now thrown out of the Garden lest they remain sinners forever by partaking of the tree of life, the couple produced children. Sin escalated. Cain flaunted a heart consumed by sin. First, he offered the unacceptable sacrifice; rejected, he sulked. God offered a correction but he refused and murdered his brother. Asked to confess, he flat out thumbed his nose against God. Judged by the Creator, he raises his fist against the judgment. Sentenced to be a restless wanderer, he built a city instead. His descendant Lamech delved into sin deeper. He also committed murder while wallowing in adultery (the first man to have two wives simultaneously!). He also raised his fist against any judgment. Sin expands. Lend an ear to what God actually said. The Holy Spirit inspired Moses to write these very words about great wickedness.

> GOD SAW THAT HUMAN EVIL WAS OUT OF
> CONTROL. PEOPLE THOUGHT EVIL,
> IMAGINED EVIL—EVIL, EVIL, EVIL FROM
> MORNING TO NIGHT. GOD WAS SORRY
> THAT HE HAD MADE THE HUMAN RACE IN
> THE FIRST PLACE; IT BROKE HIS HEART. GOD
> SAID, "I'LL GET RID OF MY RUINED
> CREATION, MAKE A CLEAN SWEEP: PEOPLE,
> ANIMALS, SNAKES AND BUGS, BIRDS—THE
> WORKS. I'M SORRY I MADE THEM."
>
> GENESIS 6:5-7 (MSG)

The Flood did not solve the problem. Sin entrenched. Right after Noah offered a thanksgiving for being the remnant of the entire populace (4 couples – eight persons!), God seriously intoned that people remained evil from the time they are as young as in childhood yet He would not eliminate them through a deluge again. (Peter wrote it would be fire next time!) True enough, Noah got drunk naked and one of his sons laughed at him and broadcasted the humiliation. Centuries later, sin excludes God. Although God steadfastly showered grace to mankind in their transgressions, sin abounded. At the plain of Shinar, the tower of Babel was erected. It was man's plan that completely ignored God. Adam was blessed to be fruitful, multiply and fill the earth. Noah and his sons were given the exact same blessings. Their descendants completely ignored God and did not want to be scattered to fill the earth. God did His will. He confused the people's languages and scattered them to fill the earth.

Sin entered, escalated, expanded, entrenched and excluded God. Even after the Redeemer had completed His work at Calvary and the empty tomb, sin still holds a firm grip on unregenerate man and to some extent even to the redeemed. John testified in his first epistle that the whole world is under the sway of the evil one. The devil has influence over every facet of man's life in every part of the globe. The believers are supposedly excluded from this pressure, but aiding and abetting the enemy among Christian ranks are not uncommon. It is rare that true believers are accused of heinous crimes or great wickedness but the devil has a more subtle trick up his sleeve. The moment a Christian excludes God, it is victory for the devil. (Remember the tower of Babel!) Any talk, action, accomplishment, attitude, accoutrement, and the like that does not include God is sin. Paul made it clear-cut that since Jesus died for all, all who live must live for Him. He personally testified that the Christ was now living his life through his faith on Him who loved him and died for him.

This generation needs the Holy Spirit more than ever.

Paul wrote to the churches in the Galatian region (the very first New Testament inspired writing!) that Jesus rescued them from their present wicked age and world order in 45 AD (CE). They were delivered from their present evil age, the wicked world they live in then. They were saved from their sinful world. They were set free from their evil world. The redemption from the wicked world order was what God wanted. It was accomplished in the Lord Jesus Christ.

2017 world order is more wicked than that evil age. None of the wickedness we witness on a daily basis existed in those times. Crimes so common nowadays were unheard of during those bygone days. Lawbreakers operating in such grandiose scale in a global stage were not possible during those times. Felonious organizations flaunting their reach like tentacles of an octopus over all the continents simply was unthinkable in that era. Government officials empowered to defend the constitution and protect the citizenry are the ones breaking the laws they are sworn to uphold. Instead of keeping the public safe from law offenders, these corrupt officers are themselves the criminals victimizing the populace. Lies are commonplace and proliferate in all social media without exceptions. Readers who should know better gobble up gossips and pass on false news. Truth is no longer absolute; it is relative. Anyone who disagrees with known facts can put up an alternative. Falsehood repeated often enough and for a long period becomes the accepted truth. Truth is now subject to private interpretation. (Scriptures should not be subjected to such!) Any person can now brandish and broadcast own version contrary to even verifiable facts and steadfast truth. Isaiah prophesied of the distress of entitling evil as good and vice-versa. He further described the disturbing penchant of sanctioning darkness as light and repudiating light as darkness. Lies are evil for Satan is the father of falsehoods (Jesus said so!). All liars would be thrown in the Lake of Fire reserved for the devil and his demons to be tormented day and night for eternity (The Holy Spirit said so!). Still, lies and liars profligate as seas inundating the information age. With such great wickedness far surpassing the evils in the time of the Flood, there is even a greater need for the Holy Spirit in this generation. There is also the impending coming of the burning of elements to make way for the new earth. It is sooner now than ever before.

Thus, this generation desperately demand the Holy Spirit in the midst of all these evils. The primary work of the Holy Spirit, which is regeneration, is the foremost necessity. All preachers, evangelists foremost, must declare the whole counsel of God as the Holy Spirit outlined it in the epistle to the Romans. The congregation Paul wrote to while he was in Cenchrea had an interesting history. On the day of Pentecost when the apostles first preached the gospel of the Lord Jesus Christ, there were Jewish converts from Rome. These proselytes from paganism (worship of man-made Roman gods) to Judaism repented of their sins and were baptized that day. They also received the Holy Spirit. They stayed in Jerusalem devoted to the apostles' doctrine and fellowship with other believers. They were forced to return to

Rome when persecution against the church arose under King Herod. Later, the Jews were expelled from Rome under Emperor Claudius. The outcasts included the Christian couple Aquila and Priscilla whom Paul met. Obviously, it was from them that Paul came to know of the Roman Christians from both the Jews and Gentiles. Aquila and Priscilla joined Paul in his missionary journeys but soon departed from each other's company. The couple stayed in Corinth while Paul went to Ephesus. Much later, the couple would return to Rome. Even much later, Paul would write the epistle to the Romans mentioning the couple in his closing remarks. Paul's theological treatise of salvation should be the staple of the gospel message. It came from the Holy Spirit.

Present-day evangelists do the Holy Spirit disservice ignoring what Paul was inspired to write. The Master Himself declared that the Holy Spirit would convict sinners of sin. Therefore, Paul writes first of condemnation before justification, sanctification and glorification. God condemned everyone as sinners. (Jesus did not come to condemn but to save!) There is no contradiction. The sinner must first be confronted of his sinfulness, repent before being saved. The evangelist's message must be this condemnation first. As Jesus promised, the Holy Spirit would supply the words coming from the Father. The very first words the sinner must hear should be the condemnation coming from God. All have sinned. It is not even about individual sins although the first chapter of the epistle zeroed in on idolatry and sexual sins. Paul expounded on the sinner's identity with Adam. The postulate of Paul is that all humanity was in Adam when he committed the sin in the Garden. All have sinned with Adam. This is how the Holy Spirit convicts every human being – man, woman and child regarding sin in each person's life. Although it is correct to stress the love of God in salvation, the sinner would appreciate more this love when the sinner first come to grips of the magnitude of sin before turning to God for redemption. Jesus gave a perfect illustration of this in the parable He asked of Simon the leprous Pharisee and the sinful woman who washed His feet with perfume. Jesus hit the nail on the head when He proclaimed that the one forgiven much would love much while the one forgiven little will love little. Gospel messages unwittingly focused on the love without the condemnation produces persons that make the confession without the profession of love towards God and Lordship of Jesus. They are simply concerned with going to heaven when death comes on earth. Paul decries this as a worldly sorrow afraid of the consequences unlike the godly sorrow that leads to repentance. Godly sorrow is deeply rooted in a heart that is so overwhelmed with the sinfulness humanity committed against God in the Garden. For the Creator God gave everything good to man and called man as a 'very good' creation. He prepared a special place for man and his wife in Eden. Still, Adam and his wife turned their backs on God's goodness. They repudiated God's words and believed the serpent's lie. They accepted the enemy's mockery of God when they were told God was lying when He said, *"You shall surely die."* They disdained God's words and succumbed to the craftiness of the serpent when the thought was planted that God was keeping good from them when He commanded them not to eat of the fruit of the knowledge of good and evil. Adam and all humanity disparaged God, belittled God, rubbished God, poured scorn on God, laughed at God, vilified God. It was not mere disobedience. This is the magnitude of sin the Holy Spirit convicts every person identified with Adam. Except for the Seed of the woman, all humanity did this to God. Yet God still loved humanity. By grace (undeserved favor) He saved humanity. Grace becomes more amazing when presented after the condemnation. Grace seems cheap when man is offered salvation without the condemnation. Man must cringe with the knowledge of treating the good God so awfully. Man must regretfully turn away from sin against the good God for He has done nothing wrong against man. The Holy Spirit makes sure man realizes this before being saved. That is why evangelistic messages bypassing this truth do not come from the Holy Spirit. This generation desperately needs the Holy Spirit.

The Jewish and Roman leaders and populace disparaged Jesus, belittled Jesus, rubbished Jesus, poured scorn on Jesus, laughed at Jesus, vilified Jesus. It was not mere crucifixion. It was the great reversal. The derision of God in the Garden brought about condemnation; the derision of God in human form (Jesus) at the Cross brought redemption. This must be the message in the mouths of all those sharing the gospel. This is the primary work of the Holy Spirit as Jesus told His disciples two thousand years ago. For even today, humanity continues to disparage Immanuel (God with us), belittle Immanuel (God with us), rubbish Immanuel (God with us), pour scorn on Immanuel (God with us), laugh at Immanuel (God with us), vilify Immanuel (God with us). It will take the Omniscient, Omnipotent, Omnipresent God the Holy Spirit to convict man of sinfulness. No church, ministry, bible school, program, person, theologian, organization, denomination, seminary, system, seminar, workshop, master's degree, doctorate in divinity, discipleship, evangelism is capable of this. Only the Holy Ghost can do this!

This generation needs to hear the Holy Spirit speak of sin and the true nature of it. Paul, still in the book of Romans, would even testify to the sinfulness of sin. He would elucidate how sin uses the holy law of God to make man sin. That's how awful sin is! This generation treats sin like a bad habit that can be replaced by a good habit. This generation treats sin like a disease that can be cured by therapy. This generation treats sin like a crime that can be dealt with through reform. Only the Holy Spirit can make clear to man the dreadfulness of sin. Only the Holy Spirit can convict sinners of the appalling nature of sin totally encompassing the human heart. Paul called it slavery. Sin is a horrific bondage no human has power to get out of forever. Only the Holy Spirit using the words of God can find man guilty of terrible transgression against the good, good, good God. The gospel then offers freedom, not just forgiveness, from sin.

That completes the initial work of the Holy Spirit in conversion. Ezekiel prophesied to the exiles in Babylon this truth. The Assyrians first conquered Israel. The Babylonians would bring Judah to exile years later. This was God's judgment to the chosen people He brought out of their more than four hundred years of bondage in Egypt. He showed them loving-kindness, goodness, mercies and compassion through those years. He performed signs, wonders and miracles on their behalf. He manifested His glorious presence in their midst through the Ark of the Covenant. He gave them the Promised Land. He made them a kingdom foremost in wealth, wisdom and power. All the nations surrounding them knew that God was with them. At the height of their renown, nations feared them because of God. For all these, Israel and Judah returned waywardness and wickedness to all the goodness God had been pouring on them. Before their exile to Babylon for seventy years, God plaintively asked His beloved nation what injustice has He done to deserve such treachery from Israel and Judah. He charged them of committing two grave evils – forsaking Him, the fountain of blessings and making for themselves gods from the other nations that can do nothing for them. God through Jeremiah talked to them that what He would do although judgement Israel and Judah deserve were actually plans to prosper them and not to harm them, plans to give them sure, joyous confident expectation of a bright future. In exile, God promised that there would come a time when He would replace disobedient hearts of stone and hard-headedness with hearts sensitive to Him. He further promised putting the Holy Spirit in these new spirits to ensure their obedience. This is accomplished in every believer in Christ.

This is the Holy Spirit urgently needed in this generation. This is the Holy Spirit that will speak of the identity of Christ in each believer. In the same manner that all humanity was identified with that awful sin of Adam in the Garden, all believers are identified with the awesome work of Christ at the Cross and Resurrection. Just as the entire human race was separated from God because of that terrible disregard of God in the Garden, all believers are reconciled to God by grace through faith in the Lord Jesus Christ. It is the work of the Holy Spirit fulfilling the prophecy of Ezekiel to all those who would believe.

This is the Holy Spirit needed in this generation. This goes beyond religious fervor and posturing, animated shouting and unintelligible garble, holiness talk and garb, theatrical performances to exhibit miracles, revival of dreams and fulfilment of fantasies. It is and must be the Holy Ghost! There is no other way as Jesus is the Way, the Truth and the Life. After all, the Holy Ghost is called the Spirit of Jesus and the Spirit of Truth.

AND REMIND THEM OF THIS: RESPECT THE RULERS
AND THE COURTS. OBEY THEM. BE READY TO DO
WHAT IS GOOD AND HONORABLE. DON'T TEAR
DOWN ANOTHER PERSON WITH YOUR WORDS.
INSTEAD, KEEP THE PEACE, AND BE CONSIDERATE. BE
TRULY HUMBLE TOWARD EVERYONE BECAUSE THERE
WAS A TIME WHEN WE, TOO, WERE FOOLISH,
REBELLIOUS, AND DECEIVED—WE WERE SLAVES TO
SENSUAL CRAVINGS AND PLEASURES; AND WE SPENT
OUR LIVES BEING SPITEFUL, ENVIOUS, HATED BY
MANY, AND HATING ONE ANOTHER. BUT THEN
SOMETHING HAPPENED: GOD OUR SAVIOR AND HIS
OVERPOWERING LOVE AND KINDNESS FOR
HUMANKIND ENTERED OUR WORLD; HE CAME TO
SAVE US. IT'S NOT THAT WE EARNED IT BY DOING
GOOD WORKS OR RIGHTEOUS DEEDS; HE CAME
BECAUSE HE IS MERCIFUL. HE BROUGHT US OUT OF
OUR OLD WAYS OF LIVING TO A NEW BEGINNING
THROUGH THE WASHING OF REGENERATION; AND
HE MADE US COMPLETELY NEW THROUGH THE HOLY
SPIRIT, WHO WAS POURED OUT IN ABUNDANCE
THROUGH JESUS THE ANOINTED, OUR SAVIOR.

TITUS 3:1-6 (VOICE)

This is the work of the Holy Spirit. It is not the work of reform school or bible school. It is not the work of Sunday school or daily vacation bible school. It is not the work of educational institutions or religious congregations. It is not the work of a democratic government allowing free speech and individual expression to gain respect or of a totalitarian government dominating the will of the people to gain the same respect. It is not learned good manners and right conduct or practiced civility of ladies and gentlemen. It is not a culture of moderation or rule of abstention from vices. It is the power of the gospel and the work of the Holy Ghost.

The last chapter of the pastoral epistle of Paul to Titus culminates the instruction of the apostle to his missionary companion left in the island of Crete. He assigned Titus to appoint elders in every city in Crete (around 100 cities!) in less than a year. Titus was to choose church leaders from among Cretans described as total liars, brute beasts and lazy gluttons. To compound the problem the island was also teeming with Judaizers who demand that gentile Christians be circumcised and be conformed to the Mosaic Law to be considered true disciples (Titus himself was an uncircumcised Greek!). In this hostile and contrary environment, Titus was tasked to achieve the impossible by simply trusting the gospel. It is the work of the Holy Ghost.

This generation needs this Holy Ghost. Too often, church growth depends on programs and procedures copied from an originator and passed on to others copiously. The system must be minutely done systematic without deviation to duplicate the original success. Believers are processed into regimens and requirements to qualify. They have to stick to the formula to mature and be delegated to lead. They must faithfully accomplish every step to the ladder of headship; then, repeat the route for others to follow. They must master the method to graduate and commence the activity in their own locality.

The Holy Ghost acts in absolute spontaneity and freedom. The Holy Ghost came upon Jesus in the Jordan baptism light as a dove fluttering without fanfare. The Holy Ghost came upon the disciples in Pentecost as divided tongues of fire following a sound from heaven like mighty rushing wind. The Holy Ghost filled the believers and they all spoke in other tongues. The Holy Ghost supplied the words the disciples had no previous knowledge. The onlookers were able to identify their mother tongues spoken by Galileans in Jerusalem. This was the very first miracle after Jesus departed. The Holy Ghost ushered His coming by the miracle of speaking in other tongues.

This is the mighty Holy Spirit needed by this generation. John would speak of the Holy Spirit as the Greater One. He is greater than the one who is in the evil world system. He is in every believer. Every member of the Body of Christ has the Holy Spirit. It does not matter what denomination the believer belongs to or what church the believer attends, every believer has the Holy Spirit needed by this generation.

The Holy Ghost is the Greater One indwelling all believers. Too often, misplaced theology and denominational beliefs confine this Greater One to healings and blessings. The Holy Ghost is misconstrued as only applicable to miracles of healings and provisions. The Holy Ghost is conveniently boxed in as the Helper to answer faith prayers and to manifest the reality of impossible requests and sometimes even mundane ones. (After all, one should not wait for the big one when not yet accustomed to little requests like simply a lost key!) He is expected to minister needs cried out in the Name of Jesus. He is testified as bringing relief in desperate times and comfort in distressing situations. He is always on time and never late to rescue God's beloved children. Money shows up exactly when needed even in the most trying times and through extra-ordinary means. Surely, He is greater than the one in control of the world system of bankrupt economy and cursed earth.

The Holy Ghost is greater in a singular way that ties up all miracles, signs and wonders in one huge lump. In the Garden, the serpent's objective was to make man fall into sin. The strategy has not changed. When sin entered the world, death in every form was born. Sickness leads to death, poverty leads to death, ignorance leads to death, greed leads to death, discrimination leads to death, self-preservation leads to death. Everything and anything not of God leads to death. Sin ushered that principle. But the principle of the Holy Spirit life sets believers free from the principle of sin and death. Thus, the Holy Ghost in every believer is greater than the tempter.

This is the Holy Ghost needed by this generation – the Holy Ghost helping man not to fall to sin and all the distresses that follows.

GIVE PRAISE TO THE GOD WHO IS ABLE TO KEEP YOU FROM FALLING INTO SIN. HE WILL BRING YOU INTO HIS HEAVENLY GLORY WITHOUT ANY FAULT. HE WILL BRING YOU THERE WITH GREAT JOY. GIVE PRAISE TO THE ONLY GOD OUR SAVIOR. GLORY, MAJESTY, POWER AND AUTHORITY BELONG TO HIM. GIVE PRAISE TO HIM THROUGH JESUS CHRIST OUR LORD. HIS PRAISE WAS BEFORE ALL TIME, CONTINUES NOW, AND WILL LAST FOREVER. AMEN.

JUDE 24-25 (NIRV)

Chapter Two
When the Holy Spirit Shows Up

THE RUACH (WIND, SPIRIT) BLOWS WHERE IT WISHES, AND THE SOUND OF IT YOU HEAR, BUT YOU DO NOT HAVE DA'AS OF WHERE IT COMES FROM AND WHERE IT GOES [KOHELET 11:5]; SO IT IS WITH EVERYONE HAVING BEEN BORN OF THE RUACH HAKODESH. [YECHEZKEL 37:9]

JOHN 3:8 (OJB)

Kohelet in English is Ecclesiastes while *Yechezkel* is Ezekiel. The preacher-author of Ecclesiastes also talked about man not being able to know the way of the wind or spirit akin to the mystery of life formed in the mother's womb or the working of the Creator God in making everything. In the miracle of the dry bones coming to life, God commanded Ezekiel to prophesy to the bones in the valley that the four winds may bring breath to them that they may live. Jesus took both these words from Scriptures to explain to Nicodemus, a teacher of Scriptures, what being born of the Spirit is all about. As Nicodemus is familiar with the fact that the Hebrew word for wind and Spirit is the same, Jesus pointed out that the invisible wind can be likened to the invisible God the Holy Spirit that brings about rebirth of the human spirit, a complete conundrum to human logic and reason used to unravel puzzling enigmas. Just as the wind cannot be seen but the effects of its movement felt and observed, the move of the Holy Spirit in the spirit born of God may be invisible but the changed life would be obvious. The new creation cannot remain odious or obnoxious once the Holy Spirit shows up in the human spirit. Apologists of Christian behavior bordering being immorally insane (if not criminally so) explain away the unchanged character as default human behavior. They equate it to the programming of the computer that unless updated, upgraded or personalized will revert to the default factory settings. In the case of humans, it is called the sinful nature. The convert naturally will act the former behavior when confronted by similar events in the past. Even if already a believer the reaction for getting hurt is retaliation since that has been ingrained in human nature before the new birth. The shepherd of such a convert with obvious anger management issues will shield the vengeful member of the church as a carnal Christian or a babe in Christ not mature enough to submit to God's word that vengeance is His and He will recompense or to repay evil with good. The pastor will be apologetic to contend that the aggressor is but a Christian and not yet a disciple.

Another stream of thought propounds the dual nature of Christians. It is religious schizophrenia. The believer purportedly has two distinct natures – the divine nature from God and the sinful nature still attached to Satan; thus, the believer has two fathers at the same time – God as Father and Satan as the other father. Jesus distinguished Himself from the Jews who believed Him. He pointedly related Himself to God as His Father and the Jews as having Satan as their father. *You are of your father, the devil.*" He minced no words declaring this. Proponents of dualism even point out to the schizophrenic nature of Christ Himself. In the account of the stilling of the waves and the wind, preachers proclaim that Jesus asleep in the boat was 100% human. When He stood up to rebuke the wind and the waves and both obeyed, He was 100% God. After that miracle, He reverted to being human again. Such obvious oddity is what is practiced by Christians that are so godly in Sunday services and so ungodly the day after. The weekdays are observed under the influence of the world; the weekends are reserved for God. (It is a Jekyll and Hyde existence inconsistent with the new creation.) Again, the inevitable excuse is that these schizophrenic Christians are not yet full-pledged disciples.

Yet if the biblical storyline is to be followed, the disciples were already disciples before they were referred to as Christians. (At least the gentile believers associated with Christ, the Greek term; the Hebrews preferred Messiah.) As delineated in the previous chapter, The Holy Ghost is able to convict sinners of their sinfulness; how much more now a believer indwelt by the same Holy Ghost. Paul argues that anyone coming to Christ by the word and the Holy Spirit will continue in the word and the Holy Spirit. Peter spoke exactly of the same theme that those born of the incorruptible word of God should desire the pure milk of the word in order to grow and mature as a genuine follower and learner of Jesus. Jesus Himself issued that evangel (good news) when He called on all those weary and burdened with sin and worldly living to come to Him and receive eternal rest for their souls. He punctuated the lesson that coming to Him necessitated learning of Him, His humility and meekness. He rebuked the Pharisees and scribes of His generation that diligently study Scriptures believing to obtain eternal life but refused to come to Him of whom the entire Scriptures testified. After his resurrection, He did a crash course with the two disciples on the road to Emmaus and explained to them starting from Moses that He is the Messiah. This ignorance prompted the Christ to command the disciples before He ascended to heaven to remain in Jerusalem for the Promise (the Holy Spirit). He charged them not to begin telling others yet until the Holy Spirit came and filled them with power from heaven. By reckoning, this would be forty days after these disciples received the Holy Spirit on Resurrection Sunday. They were inhibited to be witnesses of Jesus before they were fully equipped with power from on high. The Holy Spirit was to endue them with dynamic, explosive power to proclaim life-changing good news. Indeed, clothed with power brought about by the baptism of the Holy Spirit, the disciples preached and harvested 3000 souls that first day. Filled with the Holy Spirit, the disciples defied the Sanhedrin's decree not to preach Jesus in Jerusalem. Boldly (these same disciples were fearfully hiding from the Jews when Jesus was crucified until Jesus resurrected!), they proclaimed the gospel and harvested another 4000 souls. Daily, people were added to their number. Signs, wonders and miracles accompanied their preaching and praying. The Holy Spirit showed up every time.

The Holy Spirit showed up in Saul the least likely candidate for first king of united Israel. Saul was born in Gibeah. This place played a prominent role in the book of Judges. Wicked men of this place wanted to have sex with a passing Levite taken into an old man's house rather than stay in the town square for the town was known as corrupt. The Levite's concubine when offered in place of the Levite was raped and abused throughout the night until dawn. The eleven tribes declared war on Benjamin when that tribe refused to give up the evildoers. Benjamin was almost annihilated and ceased to be one of the tribes due to the acts of the men of Gibeah. Saul came from this place and this tribe. Years later, Hosea would speak of Gibeah as the starting point of the transgressions of Israel against God. Yet the Holy Spirit came upon Saul and he prophesied before he was anointed king. The Holy Spirit showed up in Saul in power and he defeated the Ammonites besieging Jabesh Gilead.

When Saul was rejected as king and David was anointed to take his place, Saul sought to murder David. At one time David aided by his wife Michal (Saul's daughter) escaped to Ramah the hometown of Samuel, the prophet who anointed Saul king. Saul sent soldiers to capture David but they met Samuel and the other prophets and the Holy Spirit came upon them all and they all prophesied. Three times Saul sent soldiers and the Holy Spirit came three times upon the soldiers and they prophesied with the prophets. Finally, Saul himself went to Naioth at Ramah where David hid. The Holy Spirit came upon him on the road to Naioth and he prophesied until he reached the place. In Samuel's presence Saul stripped off his royal robes and prophesied all day and night. The Holy Spirit showed up, stalled Saul's scheme, and protected David.

Supernatural occurrences accompany the showing up of the Holy Spirit. While David was a fugitive from Saul and hiding in Ziklag, the Holy Spirit came upon Amasai with those from Benjamin (Saul's relatives!) and Judah (David's relatives) and joined David in defiance of the king. The Holy Spirit came upon Azariah and he prophesied over King Asa. Encouraged by the prophet's words, the king removed the abominable idols in the southern kingdom and restored the Lord's altar. All Judah and Benjamin along with Ephraim, Manasseh and Simeon gathered to King Asa of Judah even from the northern kingdom of Israel for the people believed God was with Asa. No war erupted from that time on in the kingdom under the rule of Asa. In Ezekiel's vision, The Holy Spirit lifted up the prophet above the land and into the sky and transported him to Jerusalem then again to Chaldea. Twice this supernatural occurrence happened to the same prophet by the same Holy Ghost. Daniel was known as a wise man in whom the Holy Spirit is. Both Nebuchadnezzar and Belshazzar found out the interpretation of dreams and visions from Daniel. The seer Hanani spoke of God showing up strong on behalf of those who are faithful.

The Holy Ghost shows up even in the most unseemingly inopportune time. Ananias and Sapphira found this out. Peter pronounced judgment to the couple who dared lie to God the Holy Spirit. The wife did not even have time to mourn her recently deceased husband; she followed him to death right after (two hours hence!). Endless speculations have been proposed as to that act of the Holy Spirit adding no lucid clarity to the situation. Even more arguments rise as to whether the two were genuine believers and if they ended up in heaven or hell. In the hermeneutical principle of staying on the line teaching that no one should add or subtract from the text presented, the simple answer as to where the couple ended is quite clear in the narrative. They were buried so they ended up in the ground. Anything beyond that is conjecture and assumption. Systematic theology suggests to compare this incidents with God's judgment on Nadab and Abihu, on Achan and on Uzzah. Death was swift to come to these Old Testament characters. Drawing this parallel, it is suggested that the couple were pretenders not schizophrenic (as previously discussed). Proponents of this view point to the verse that Satan filled Ananias' heart in the same way that happened to Judas the night he betrayed Jesus. They also connect this view with the verse Luke testified to that *'no one else dared join them'* even if God daily added to their number more and more believers. The showing up of the Holy Spirit in that incident frightened pretenders and halfhearted followers to risk life and limb lying to the Holy Ghost. The conspiracy to connive to deceive the Holy Spirit was dealt with severely in order to leave no doubt that the Holy Spirit will not tolerate hypocrisy and pretense. Peter accused the wife of putting the Holy Spirit to test calling to mind the wilderness journey of the first generation Israelites (more than 600,00 men 20 years old and above) set free from bondage to Egypt constantly complaining and griping against God for forty years. They all died in the desert.

This story is a sober reminder of when the Holy Spirit shows up. Israel remembers.

I will mention the steadfast love of the Lord and the praises of the Lord, according to all that the Lord has bestowed on us, and the great goodness toward the house of Israel, which He has bestowed on them according to His mercy, and according to the multitude of His kindnesses. For He said, "Surely they are My people, sons who will not lie." So He became their Savior. In all their affliction He was afflicted, and the angel of His presence saved them; in His love and in His mercy He redeemed them; and He lifted them and carried them all the days of old. But they rebelled and grieved His Holy

Spirit; therefore, He turned Himself to be their enemy, and He
fought against them.

Then His people remembered the days of old, of Moses, saying:
Where is He who brought them up out of the sea with the
shepherds of His flock? Where is He who put His Holy Spirit in their
midst, who led them with His glorious arm by the right hand of
Moses, dividing the water before them, to make Himself an
everlasting name, who led them through the deep, as a horse in
the wilderness, that they should not stumble? As the cattle which
go down into the valley, the Spirit of the Lord caused them to rest,
so You led Your people, to make Yourself a glorious name.
Isaiah 63:7-14 (MEV)

Paul reminded the Christians in his era of the same two things in
response to all God has done for them in the Lord Jesus Christ and
by the Holy Spirit. He admonished them to stop lying to each other
for they are members of one another and to heed not to grieve the
Holy Spirit, the guarantee of redemption.

The Holy Spirit does show up supernaturally sometimes preferred
spectacularly. Paul filled with the Holy Spirit and incensed by a
sorcerer's attempt to prevent the proconsul from being a Christian
declared blindness to Elymas, a Jewish false prophet also known
as Bar-Jesus. He sought to bar Sergius Paulus from professing
Jesus as Lord and Savior. Paul called out the Jew as son of the
devil, enemy of righteousness, deceitful and fraudulent in

perverting the ways of God even in his professed Judaism. For it was the proconsul who arranged to meet Paul and company to hear from them the word of God personally. That dramatic turn of events where the false prophet turned blind convinced Sergius Paulus in his astonishment at the power of the Holy Spirit to believe the good news.

Definitely something is bound to happen when the Holy Ghost shows up. Stephen full of the Holy Spirit in front of his detractors, a lynch mob primed for murder, looked up and saw the glorious God with Jesus at His right hand. He testified to the crowd what the Holy Spirit had shown him and was promptly stoned to death. Simon the sorcerer saw Pete and John lay hands on believers to receive the Holy Ghost and offered money for such ability (as the magician called it unaware of the supernatural move). He was rebuked. Ananias laid hands on Saul (blind for three days after meeting Jesus on the road to Damascus) and something like scales fell from Saul's eyes and his sight was restored after being filled with the Holy Ghost. The Holy Spirit encouraged Peter to not hesitate to go with Cornelius' men after seeing the vision of a large sheet coming down from heaven full of unclean animals. While yet preaching to Cornelius' household, the Holy Spirit came on all who heard the message. They were baptized in the Holy Spirit before being baptized in water. The Holy Spirit told the gathering of prophets and teachers in the church at Antioch to separate Barnabas and Saul for their missionary journeys. The Holy Spirit directed their way to Cyprus crossing Salamis all the way to

Paphos. The Holy Spirit filled the disciples with joy even as they were persecuted and expelled from the region of Pisidian Antioch. At Iconium, they spoke boldly under the unction of the Holy Spirit even under threats of mistreatment and stoning to death. They fled to the surrounding country to continue to preach the good news. At Ephesus, the church was birthed from twelve disciples after they received baptism of the Holy Ghost when Paul placed his hands on them. The Holy Spirit even showed up healing the sick touched by handkerchiefs and aprons previously touched by Paul. Evil spirits were also expelled from them. The prophet Agabus from Judea took Paul's belt and prophesied by the Holy Spirit that the owner of the belt will be tied up by the Jews in Jerusalem. Paul had already mentioned this on his farewell address to the Ephesian elders informing them that he was compelled by the Holy Spirit to go to Jerusalem where prison and hardships await him.

Truly things are stirred up upon the arrival of the Holy Ghost. Men are moved and circumstances changed when the Holy Spirit shows up. Adverse conditions are reversed. Revelations flow freely. Prophecies are spoken. Miracles, signs and wonders abound. The devil and his demons are cast out. The works of the devil are undone. The Holy Spirit restores. Now all these should be welcomed good tidings and should result in rejoicings among the people. True enough, testimonies of exultations and praises to God occur in these acts of the Holy Spirit; but contrary reactions also surface. Mocking, death threats and actual killings, persecutions also arise. Nevertheless, whatever the response may be (be it adversarial or acquiescence), the truth remains – the Holy Spirit shows up and something happens.

Paul enlightened the Corinthians on the manifestations gifts brought about by the Holy Spirit on every believer for the benefit of all. Vocal gifts, power gifts, and revelation gifts abound and are dispensed as the Holy Spirit wills. He operates these gifts for the goal to edify, encourage and comfort the church at large and individual members in particular. The believers are exhorted to be zealous regarding these gifts. They are to pursue the best gifts for the moment – that is which gift is needed for the situation. The gifts are not for bragging but so that the Holy Spirit can bring about the essential equipment of the hour. The Holy Spirit is that way. Jesus testified that the Mighty Holy Spirit will not magnify Self but direct everyone to the Christ. He is not going take on anything of His own but only take on what is of the Christ. Such is the situation every time the Holy Spirit shows up. He heightens the accomplished work and ongoing ministry of the Lord Jesus Christ. He does not broadcast Self but reveals more of Jesus to both the believers and the unbelieving world. He also uncovers the purposes and plans of God for the individual believer and the entire Body of Christ. He makes known things to come for the individual believer and the entire Body of Christ. He brings to light darkened understanding and illumines mind to the truth.

Thousands of years have passed since the first time the Holy Spirit showed up in Creation, are there still lingering questions of His showing up for whatever He wills to do? Is He bound by the laws of nature or the faith of believers? Is He limited in His acts of wisdom and power? Can anything or anyone stop Him? What can hinder His showing up? What can be beyond His ability?

The Holy Spirit shows up. Expect the unexpected. He is not programmable.

Chapter 3

The Stirring of the Spirit Before the Advent of Christ

In this chapter, we will focus on The Holy Spirit during the time of the Iron Age or, in keeping with biblical chronology, the period of time in the Old Testament prior to the Advent of Christ.

This timeframe captures the years from 1200 BC to 586 BC.

To begin our journey, it is meaningful to realize and appreciate that The Spirit of God is mentioned in the Old Testament 75 times. Interestingly enough, The Spirit of God is mentioned with the terms of your Spirit, The Spirit of God, The Spirit of the Lord, My Spirit, The Spirit, The Spirit of God, and The Spirit of a "particular quality". Those qualities could include judgment, fire, justice, etc. The actual title of The Holy Spirit is only mentioned three times.

From His presence and activity in the Old Testament we can take away a number of valuable teachings.

Specifically, we will be reminded of His wonderful role in creation and realize the characteristics of His tenderness. Secondly, we will open our hearts and embrace the personality of God's Spirit. Finally, we will be energized through a brief study of his magnificent power and thrill once again of His promised presence in the lives of believers.

The Work of the Holy Spirit in Creation

In Genesis 1:2, (KJV) we read that "The Spirit of God moved upon the face of the waters." Moved, in the Hebrew dictionary, is the word *rachaph*. The Hebrew translation for the word moved is to shake, move, or flutter. The word *rachaph* also draws upon the illustration of a dove or hovering dove that broods or watches over its young.

As we meditate on the "movement" of The Holy Spirit, our hearts continue to be overwhelmed as we think of the implications of just this one word as it relates to the work of The Holy Spirit in creation. We are immediately impressed with the reality that The Spirit of God is a dynamic entity, indeed a dynamic personality. Movement is a verb and it can be argued that movement is the pure definition of life.

Additionally, His presence is active as indicated by the word shake. This word shake, as denoted in the word *rachaph,* immediately transports us to the Acts of the Apostles as seen in chapter 4:31 (KJV), "And when they had prayed, the place was shaken when they were assembled together; and they were all filled with the Holy Ghost, and they spake the word of God with boldness."

The Spirit of God shakes "things up." Whether those things are people or situations, when The Spirit of God is present, things are never the same.

Above all, the movement of The Holy Spirit speaks to our hearts about tenderness and watchfulness over His creation. For the word *rachaph* denotes a loving care over that which has been created by The Creator.

And so the presence of The Holy Spirit at creation reveals to our hearts that He is real, He is powerful, He reveals Himself through activity and that His presence causes extraordinary and powerful movement in a loving way.

Before the the works of The Holy Spirit during this timeframe are studied, it is imperative to embrace, appreciate and reflect on the personality of God The Holy Spirit.

The Personality of The Holy Spirit

In Genesis the second chapter, we read that God stated it is not good that man should be alone. Therefore, it is safe to assert that God understands the need for His creation to have fellowship. It would also be a safe assertion to realize that God the Creator wants to have fellowship with His creation. This desire for God to have fellowship is seen in Genesis 3:9 (KJV) as God came walking in the garden and called out to Adam and said, "Where art thou?"

As with any relationship, the pitfall and subsequent deterioration of a union can be fractured due to a number of reasons. Some of those reasons could include actions that can create distrust, selfishness, unfaithfulness, etc.

Additionally, more often than not, an initial relationship can be soured if that partnership is based on "what can you do for me?" Everything is fine in the relationship especially when those selfish expectations are met. However, if the relationship is based solely upon what one person can do for another the result can become splintered and damaged when those expectations are not met.

A prime example of a period of time set aside to know one another in a relationship is known as being engaged. An engagement is a set upon period of time where the couple begins to talk, spend time with one another and build trust in each other in order to understand who the other person is and then building a relationship based upon compatibility.

The same can be paralleled when it comes to establishing and progressing in a relationship with God through the atonement of Christ and the wonderful presence of His Holy Spirit.

To illustrate the importance of a relationship, there is a story told where hundreds had congregated in an auditorium. They had come to see and more importantly hear an extraordinary Shakespearean actor who was well-versed in making oratory come alive. His speech was skillful as he enunciated his every syllable in a masterful way.

After performing Shakespeare for awhile, he wished to engage the audience and asked the crowd if anyone had a particular passage from one of the Shakespeare plays or some other popular verbal passage that they would like him to express. From the back of the room one older gentleman stood and asked the great orator if he would recite the 23rd Psalm. The famous orator said that he would if the elderly gentleman would agree to recite the same passage following his performance.

As one can imagine, the 23rd Psalm was recited perfectly. The great orator captured the essence of the Psalm as well as using his diction training to perfectly enunciate every line and syllable and matching the proper inflection of tone during his recital.

Following the recitation, the crowd showed their delight and appreciation by standing for the presentation and performer and offering a thunderous ovation for the performance well done.

After the crowd quieted down, the elderly man came to the front of the auditorium and true to his word, began reciting the 23rd Psalm. His voice betrayed his age as it cracked and quivered. However, undaunted, he began with the first line of the 23rd Psalm (KJV) "The Lord is my shepherd, I shall not want."

Following his sharing of this famous Psalm, he then sat down. For this elderly man there was no standing ovation and there was no applause given. And yet, on the faces and in the eyes of each of those who heard this moving account of the shepherd's prayer and praise, streamed tears of inspiration and rapture reflected on the faces of those who listened.

Baffled by what they had just witnessed, one of the audience members asked the extraordinary orator what happened, what had they just witnessed? Why was the response of the audience different when both men recited the same passage?

The Shakespearean actor looked at the elderly audience member, through tears in his own eyes, and simply stated, "I know how to recite the 23rd Psalm, but that man knows the shepherd and that makes all the difference in the world."

Would that we not only know God's Word, but The God of The Word.

The personality of The Holy Spirit can also be grieved. Isaiah 63:10 (NIV) states, "Yet they rebelled and grieved his Holy Spirit. So he turned and became their enemy and he himself fought against them." Obviously, we too can grieve The Holy Spirit if we do not listen to His instruction, obey His commands, follow His leading or if we commit other acts of rebellion. In doing so not only do we grieve The Holy Spirit, but we ourselves become vessels that cannot be fully utilized to bring glory to God.

Also, during David's prayer of contrition, as seen in Psalms 51, David prays and asks that God will not take His Holy Spirit from him. Depending upon your theology and interpretation of The Scriptures this can either denote that The Spirit of God can leave a believer or that sin can mask the powerful presence and usefulness of God in our lives. In either case, The Holy Spirit has basically departed.

Finally, when it comes to the personality of The Holy Spirit it is incredibly breathtaking to realize that we can never fully understand the depth of The Triune God. In Isaiah 40:13 (KJV) we read, "Who hath directed the Spirit of the Lord, or being his counselor have taught him." In other words, who among us can give The Spirit of God advice or teach Him about life or provide insight or instruction to Him as to how things should be. Therefore,

He is the ultimate teacher and instructor and He has all the answers. Indeed, The Triune God is the answer for all of life's questions and perplexities. Consequently, to realize that He indwells the New Testament believer is an incredible reality to be embraced and appreciated...even if He chooses to be silent in response to our questions.

The Power of The Holy Spirit

In regards to our focus or concentration on the works of The Holy Spirit of God, it is important to understand that in the Old Testament, during this time period, The Holy Spirit did not indwell the believer. However, The Spirit of God came mightily upon both men and women to provide a certain quality of leadership, to strengthen the chosen of God to perform a certain action, to endow the individual with God's wisdom, to teach a Spiritual lesson, to give Spiritual insight, etc.

This temporary empowerment by The Spirit of God was necessary as God always has a plan, but His plan generally includes partnership with an individual or entity. This cooperation to achieve God's plan is clearly indicated in Ezekiel 22:30 (KJV), "And I sought for a man among them that should make up the hedge, and stand in the gap before me for the land, that I should not destroy it: but I found none."

Also, true to God's grace, the men and women that God chose for a special dispensation in the Old Testament did not need to be perfect. Indeed, many were flawed and disobedient in their relationship with God. These less-than-perfect vessels used by God can be clearly seen in the likes of Samson who clearly had an eye for women, David who was a murderer and adulterer and even Moses who was disobedient and smote the rock rather than speaking to the rock.

It is also important to note, unlike the work of the same Holy Spirit in the New Testament, once that particular action was satisfied and God was glorified, The Spirit of God departed. The departure of The Spirit from a chosen individual is clearly seen in the person of Saul as seen in I Samuel 16:14 (KJV), "But the Spirit of the Lord departed from Saul, and an evil Spirit from the Lord troubled him."

A prime example of the incredible power of God overshadowing a mere human being is seen in the life of Samson. As you'll recall, Samson was one of the judges that led the nation of Israel. In Judges 14:6 (KJV) we read, "And the Spirit of the Lord came mightily upon him, and he rent him as he would have rent a kid, and he had nothing in his hand: but he told not his father or his mother what he had done." In this particular verse we are reminded that the anointed of God are protected and nothing can harm them unless the Lord allows otherwise. In addition, the reality of "not by might, nor by power, but by my spirit, saith the Lord" (Zechariah 4:6) (KJV) is seen here as Samson did not have a weapon, but used his bare hands to slay the lion. In an incredible fashion we might add. It is also important to add that not only did Samson derive physical strength from The Spirit of God, but most certainly a supernatural courage as well.

Additionally, it is important to realize that God has given unto us "Power to tread on serpents and scorpions, and over all the power of the enemy: and nothing shall by any means hurt you" (Luke 10:19 KJV). Obviously, this does not mean that we pick up deadly serpents and play with scorpions, but to realize that nothing, outside of God's will, can harm us because we are in the palm of God's hand.

Also, realizing that the same Holy Spirit of the Old Testament is the same Holy Spirit of the New Testament, we see that in the Old Testament gifts were given unto God's chosen. This is seen in Exodus 31:3 (KJV) as God says, "And I have filled him with the Spirit of God, in wisdom, understanding, and knowledge, and in all manner of workmanship..." Additionally, in Numbers 11:26, we see that certain individuals were given the power of prophecy. The beauty for the believer living in the New Testament era is that, because of the presence of God's Holy Spirit indwelling us, we all have been endowed with various spiritual gifts.

Another Spiritual gift that was accorded certain individuals in the Old Testament was the gift of visions as found in Ezekiel 8:3 (KJV). This verse reads, "And he put forth the form of an hand, and took me by a lock of mine head; and the Spirit lifted me up between the earth and heaven, and brought me in the visions of God to Jerusalem, to the door of the inner gate that looketh toward the north; where was the seat of the image of jealousy, which provoketh us to jealousy."

For a moment dwell deeply upon this passage of Scripture. First of all, this was not a physical transportation of Ezekiel to the City of Jerusalem. However, it was a spiritual vision in which Ezekiel was transported to the gate by which the priests went directly to the great altar.

In this verse it is important to note that the pronoun that is used is Us. Therefore, it is safe to assume that The Us refers to the Trinity, but, could it also possibly be that The Us was including Ezekiel as he was God's prophet? This certainly speaks of our unity with God and the fact that what God loves we love, what God hates we hate and what provokes God to jealousy should be what provokes us to jealousy as well. Many commentators believe that the jealousy referred to in this Scripture verse is God's reaction to the idolatry that is taking place in Jerusalem.

And so, the question needs to be asked, because of our union with God through His Spirit, do we find ourselves angry at what God is angry at and do we find ourselves loving as God loves and do we find ourselves grieved over that which grieves Him? This is important to determine especially in the matters of spirituality and sin.

The Spirit of God, in the Old Testament, also provided guidance and leadership in certain situations and through certain individuals. An example of the leading of The Holy Spirit is seen in Isaiah 63:11-14 (KJV). These verses read, "Then he remembered the days of old, Moses, and his people, saying, where is he that brought them up out of the sea with the shepherd of his flock? Where is he that put his Holy Spirit within him? That led them by the right hand of Moses with his glorious arm, dividing the water before them, to make himself an everlasting name? That led them through the deep, as an horse in the wilderness, that they should not stumble? As a beast goeth down into the valley, the Spirit of the Lord caused him to rest: so didst thou lead us thy people, to make himself a glorious name."

In this particular verse, we see that the leading of God is a leading out of danger for His people. The verse also talks about leading His people out of the wilderness like a horse being led from that which is barren or the desert. Also, wonderfully, God leads His people into the valley. That valley is a place of respite and rest so that God can be glorified. Please remember that God does not promise to keep us from the deserts or wildernesses of life, but for a purpose, he brings us through those experiences so that we can bring glory to His Name.

As we meditate on the spiritual rest that God provides for the believer, Isaiah 63:14 (KJV), "As a beast goeth down into the valley, the Spirit of the Lord caused him to rest: so didst thou lead thy people, to make thyself a glorious name", it is glorious for the believer to comprehend the gift of rest by God's Spirit.

One aspect of this rest is the relief from being burdened by sin and our sin nature. We no longer need to carry the shame, disgrace and ugliness of those things that we have done. The rest, through God's Spirit, is a freedom from not only sin, but He gives us His rest from the consequences of a guilty conscience. We are at rest from our sins and sin nature.

Another aspect or spiritual benefit to receiving The Spirit of rest is that we no longer need to strive to do good works to please God. God is only pleased through the finished work of His son Jesus Christ whom we have union with. Be not mistaken, however, because of the Spirit of God within us we will accomplish good works for His glory and honor.

Another example of His leading is found in Psalm 25:9 (NIV). That verse reads "He guides the humble in what is right and teaches them his way." Here God's promise is clearly asserted in that He promises to guide and teach. However, the promise can only be a reality if the individual themselves come to God in humility and with a humble Spirit. The individual's prayer for guidance should be, "Lord, I have no idea of what to do or where to go, but you have promised to show me, guide me and lead me. I place myself into your hands unreservedly. Thank you!"

Also, the power of The Spirit is demonstrated through His anger. In Ephesians 4:26 (KJV) we are amazed with the words, "Be ye angry, and sin not: let not the sun go down on your wrath:" This is an amazing verse in that often times we are taught not to be angry. This anger, as seen in this New Testament verse, is the Greek word *orgizo*. It literally means to provoke or enrage or become exasperated or be angry.

In fact, not only does God get angry in the Old Testament, but there was an instance when The Spirit of God came upon Saul and Saul became angry. This is found in I Samuel 11:6 (KJV), "And the Spirit of God came upon Saul when he heard these tidings and his anger was kindled greatly." Obviously, through this verse, we see that when The Spirit of God came upon Saul he became angry. This was over a threat issued by an Ammonite by the name of Nahash.

And so, as believers, when we see the state of the church or look upon the circumstances that are happening in the world around us, it is important to know that God may cause us to be angry. Therefore, we should be angry at what angers God. However, the key is not to sin. Some Biblical commentators attribute this sin to be an attitude of the believer when anger rises up within because the individual believer's feelings have been hurt or they have been wronged rather than being angry at the things, attitudes, events, etc. that anger God.

It seems that in each historical era there are challenges that are faced by the faithful during this time. Indeed, our current issues around the globe today testify to the reality that there will always be problems. Basically these problems or challenges that are faced are of the global community's own doing.

The same can be said to be true during each of the historical eras as recorded for us in the Old Testament. However, it appears, that God always intervened. He intervened in a number of ways by endowing certain people with gifts and powers so that miracles or certain actions could be performed by His Spirit. The Spirit resting on these leaders happened so that they could respond to the challenges of the day by inspiring and leading God's people.

One of the qualities of The Spirit that was demonstrated to empower those leaders that were chosen was through the giving of The Spirit of Wisdom. So often, we think that we have the answers based upon our own education, experience, personal know-how, and our own wisdom in which we think that we can lead the people and the nation in a quality way.

However, as it was in years gone by so it is today. We need The Spirit of Wisdom that far exceeds the intellect or wisdom of mankind. It is the Wisdom of God that is needed to govern, to lead and to inspire those leaders who have been called to lead. This Wisdom, as Solomon prayed for, is seen in Exodus 31:13 (KJV), " And I have filled him with the spirit of God, in wisdom, and in understanding, and in knowledge, and in all manner of workmanship" and in Exodus 28:3 (KJV), "And thou shalt speak unto all that are wise hearted, whom I have filled with the spirit of wisdom."

Finally, when it comes to the power of God it is important to realize that effective, meaningful and God glorifying power is His and His alone. In other words, the believer cannot accomplish God's work in their own strength or by their own wisdom. They must rely wholly and totally upon God himself.

This is clearly seen in Psalm 127:1 (KJV). That verse exclaims, "Except the Lord build the house, they labour in vain that build it: except the Lord keep the city, the watchmen waketh but in vain."

How often do we as church leaders and believers try to do the work of God in our own strength. We work and work and get tired and we do not see any fruits of our labor. This has nothing to do with the will of God or what He requires of us, but it is a matter of whose strength we are relying on. This reality of God's strength or power needed for the task at hand is made quite clear for we read in Zechariah 4:6 (KJV), "Then he answered and spake unto me, saying, This is the word of the Lord unto Zerubbabel, saying, Not by might, nor by power, but by my Spirit, saith the Lord of hosts."

Also, in regards to God's direction, Proverbs 3:5,6 (KJV) states emphatically, "Trust in the Lord with all thine heart and lean unto thine own understanding. In all thy ways acknowledge him and he will direct thy paths."

The Promised Presence of The Holy Spirit

In days gone by it was often said that a man's word was his bond. Often deals were established through the words of two individuals and sealed with a handshake.

Today that is not necessarily so.

In fact today, where the bonds of marriage are promised to each other through spoken vows, the divorce rate in United States of America is an astounding 50% or more. Also, there are the politicians promising this that and the other thing if the voter will vote for the person running for office. We all know how that goes and seldom does the politician keep their promise.

As we have concluded looking at the works of The Spirit before the advent of Christ, we have briefly observed and been amazed at His presence during creation, we have gotten to know him by exploring His dynamic personality and we have been awed by the power of The Holy Spirit.

However, Praise the Lord, this study does not end there nor does the Holy Spirit's work stop in the Old Testament. The person and the power of The Holy Spirit is not just for the yesterday's of history but promised for the believer in their today's and whatever tomorrows are granted.

Therefore, we wish to conclude this chapter by looking at the promise of God in giving the presence of His Holy Spirit to believers.

First of all, in the Old Testament, we have the promise and fulfillment of full salvation of God as seen in Isaiah 61:1 (KJV), "The Spirit of the Lord God is upon me; because the Lord hath anointed me to preach good tidings unto the meek; he hath sent me to bind up the brokenhearted, to proclaim liberty to the captives, and the opening of the prison to them that are bound;"

This verse speaks to the anointing of The Messiah, The Christ or our Lord Jesus Christ. Because of His obedience even to His death upon the cross at Calvary, we have, through his obedience, been promised The Holy Spirit. Through his death and resurrection, the outpouring of The Holy Spirit came as seen in the second Chapter of Acts.

Consequently, we have the promise, as seen in Ezekiel 36:27 (KJV). This verse reads, "And I will put my Spirit within you, and cause you to walk in my statutes, and ye shall keep my judgments, and do them."

Not only do we have the anointing of The Holy Spirit and His indwelling within us, this wonderful union enables us to walk obediently in the laws or statues of God and keep His judgments in obedience.

It's also important to note that the promise of The Holy Spirit is to all those who believe in The Lord Jesus Christ. This is clearly seen in Joel 2:29 (KJV) which reads "And also upon the servants and upon the handmaids in those days will I pour out my Spirit." Please note that there is no discrimination involved with the outpouring of The Holy Spirit. This promise and gift in the person of The Holy Spirit is to the "whosoever will may come."

In conclusion, this brief study of The Holy Spirit, as seen before the advent of Christ, teaches us a number of beautiful, memorable and splendid qualities about the personality, presence and the power of The Spirit of God and that being part of the Triune Godhead He was indeed present at creation.

It is in no way intended to be exhaustive, but certainly a brief synopsis that will hopefully draw the reader into a deeper study and in the knowledge of God The Holy Spirit.

Our next chapter will deal with specific men and women of God and how God The Holy Spirit utilized them in certain historical situations to bring Him glory and honor. Additionally, it is important to note the transformation that takes place in the believer when the power of The Holy Spirit descends. And, glory to God, He is the same Holy Spirit of the New Testament as we see in the Old Testament.

Chapter 4

Men and Women Who Lit Up the Iron Age With the Holy Ghost Fireworks

Having been introduced on a bit of a deeper scale to The Holy Spirit and made more aware or further reminded of His promises and power, we now wish to study The Spirit's impact. Consequently, we will study the backdrop or timeframe of His intervention, the impact that His presence had on the chosen vessel as well as the glorious impact that He had on the situation.

We will study a sampling of both men and women who have different roles or actions to perform. We will also see that these men and women were ordinary individuals, but when The Holy Spirit came upon them they were given certain gifts, talents or insight to be the qualified person that God needed at that particular time.

In addition, we are going to limit our timeframe of study to that era known as the Iron Age. Specifically, that time frame ranges from 1200 BC to 500 BC. As it relates to The Scripture, this period of time geographically corresponds to the men and women of faith during the Babylonian, Assyrian and Persian Empires.

Joshua

Joshua's name means Yahweh is salvation. He had a close leadership role with Moses. Additionally, he was two of 12 men that went into the land of Canaan to spy out the land and determine whether the nation of Israel could conquer the Caananites. He and Caleb came back with a positive report saying that they could conquer the land while the other 10 spies came back with a negative report.

In Numbers 27:18 through 23 we see that he was named as the successor of Moses. Joshua is known for his faith, obedience courage and devotion to the law of God.

In the book of Joshua we read that God came unto Joshua and commanded him to cross over the Jordan River and seize the land. God proclaimed that on every part of the land that the sole of his foot touched would be given unto him and the nation of Israel.

In regards to not only the Word of God coming to Joshua and Joshua believing what God had said, we also see the work of The Holy Spirit in Joshua's life.

First of all, in Numbers 27:18 (NIV) we read "Take Joshua son of Nun, a man in whom is the spirit and lay your hand on him." Therefore, we see that in order to glorify God and be successful in whatever capacity God has called that individual; His spirit needs to be upon or indwell that individual.

Additionally, in Deuteronomy 34:9, we read Joshua son of Nun was filled with The Spirit of wisdom because Moses had laid his hands on him as The Lord commanded. And so the Israelites listened to Joshua.

In this verse we can take away a number of encouragements when it comes to having the presence of The Spirit of God with us and upon us and in us. Of note is that first of all, because of The Spirit of Wisdom, those that he was about to lead and leading listened to him. This speaks of respect and the leader being inspired to instill in those he leads with the same attributes.

Another takeaway is that The Spirit in this verse is referred to as The Spirit of Wisdom. Wisdom is what Solomon asked for as the quality to lead the people of God. In Job 28:18 (KJV) we read, "For the price of wisdom is above rubies." What confidence Joshua must have had knowing that he was filled with The Spirit of Wisdom. For the Christian today, we are blessed because we have

Christ and in I Corinthians 1:24 (KJV) we read, "But unto them which are called, both Jews and Greeks, Christ the power of God, and the wisdom of God."

The life of Joshua and the leadership of Joshua, as seen in the book of Joshua, stresses the importance of God's faithfulness, the written commandments of God and God's holiness as it relates to God's dealing with His servants and with the Canaanites.

Above all, the partnership between Joshua and His God by His Spirit speaks of the power of faith in glorifying The Lord God and achieving God's will and plan for the lives of His people.

Saul

The beauty of conducting a brief study on the personality and person of Saul is that, we as individuals, can really relate to not only the times where he was at his pinnacle in being God's servant, but also relate at the revealing of his feet of clay.

In response to the people who wished for a king to lead him, God instructed Samuel to search for a king. In I Samuel 9:2 we are introduced to a young man by the name of Saul. For all intents and purposes he has the looks of a king about him. He was goodly, he was young and stood head and shoulders above those around him.

The cautionary tale here is that we need to be careful about judging based on outward appearances in regards to the leaders of God. They may be dressed well or look great and not have a hair out of place, but it is important to remember that God looks the heart. This perspective from the Lord is clearly seen in I Samuel 16:7, (KJV), "For the Lord seeth not as man seeth; for man looketh on the outward appearance, but the Lord looketh on the heart."

And so Saul is anointed as king. In I Samuel 10:6,7 (KJV) we read, "And the spirit of the Lord will come upon thee, and thou shall prophecy with them, and shall be turned into another man. And let it be, when these signs are come unto thee, that thou do as occasion serve thee; for God is with thee."

Glory to God! Here we see through the anointing of Samuel by God's direction, there are three significant takeaways from these two verses. The first take away is that as God comes upon Saul he is given the gift of prophecy. It is important to note that first of all this is a gift. There is nothing that man can do to earn this gift. It is not only a gift of The Spirit of God but it is an indication that The Spirit of God is present.

The second take away is that Saul will be turned into another man. This does not mean that his physical appearance will change. However, it does mean that his heart will be changed. He will desire the things that God desires he will love the things that God loves he will hate the things that God hates. In the New Testament, the Scripture that probably would speak to this change in Saul would be found in II Corinthians 5:17 (KJV), "Therefore if any man be in Christ, he is a new creature: old things are passed away, behold, all things are become new."

Finally, for Saul in this verse, we see that God is with him. We cannot underestimate the presence of God in our lives and with His presence comes all that He is. In fact, as you'll recall, when Moses was seeking God and asking for God to show him the way, God responded by saying, "And he said, My presence shall go with thee, and I will give thee rest" (Exodus 33:14 KJV). So often we ask God for this that or the other thing. We cry out to God, show me the way, and please bless me! And what is God's response? You have my presence; you have me. That is all you need!

On the other hand, Saul is an ideal example of a person who can be cast aside by God as well. He was chosen by God and when he was obedient to God's word, God used him mightily to beat the Ammonites. However, as Saul progressed in his leadership role so did his disobedience to God. One of the key verses in I Samuel is chapter 15:22 (KJV) when Samuel says to Saul "To obey is better than sacrifice." In this verse Samuel brings to Saul's attention that he disobeyed God by saving some of the sheep and not destroying, in its entirety, the Amalekites and their possessions.

The lesson for us as believers here is to not only obey the Word of God, but not to take possession of the world's goods. We need to be wholly set apart for The Lord.

Consequently, his fall was great as he lost a number of gifts that God had given him. Those gifts included the loss of his kingship and God's presence. In fact, we read that an evil spirit comes to him.

In addition, he takes on a jealous and wicked personality as seen in his attempted murder of David. Also, because of his unfaithfulness, his sin divides his household as seen through the betrayal of his son Jonathan. In fact he fell so far from his relationship with The Lord that he sought counsel from a witch. Eventually, he was wounded in battle and took his own life through suicide.

David

Following the reign of Saul, God sent Samuel to the house of Jesse of Bethlehem. God had instructed Samuel to go there and anoint the next king of Israel. Jesse had a total of eight sons and as each of the first seven sons passed by Jesse, God said that he had not chosen any of those sons who passed before him. It is here again that God reminds Samuel not to look on the outside, but upon the heart.

And so Samuel said, following the rejection of the seventh son, do you have any other sons? Jesse replied yes that he had a young son by the name of David and he was tending the sheep. Samuel said send for him.

When David passed by in front of Samuel, Samuel was instructed by God to rise and anoint him for he was the one. Thus we see the anointing of David by God's prophet.

It can probably be argued that of all of the Old Testament figures, David is probably the most beloved and referred to. In fact God said that David was a man after His own heart.

The first indication of God's anointing upon David was when David met Goliath on the field of battle. It would probably be a safe assumption to declare that every Christian and non-Christian has heard the story of David and Goliath. The beauty of this story between a giant and a shepherd is found in I Samuel 17:45 (NIV) when David said, "You come against me with sword and spear and javelin, but I come against you in the name of the Lord Almighty, the God of the armies of Israel, whom you have defied."

The power of the story is not lost on us as it relates to the goliaths that we face in our lives today. First of all, our weapons are not the normal weapons that the world would be considered as dangerous. This is because David was only armed with a shepherd's sling and three stones. Clearly this powerful story underscores the fact that it is by God Spirit that we are victorious over the enemies of The Lord.

Secondly, David declared that Goliath would be delivered into his hands. Is this not a powerful affirmation of faith. Faith being defined as the substance of things hoped for and the evidence of things yet not seen.

Thirdly, it can be argued that Goliath is a type of Satan. This argument is based on the fact that when God's hand guided that stone straight and true and embedded itself in the forehead of Goliath; David then took Goliath's sword and cut off the head of Goliath. This battle between good and evil or the church and Satan is clearly evidenced as we refer back to Genesis 3:15, when God, true to His word, said that the offspring of the woman would crush the head of Satan.

Because of The Holy Spirit being upon David, we also see the tenderness and integrity of David's heart. The purity of his heart can be clearly seen when Saul was in the cave which afforded him the opportunity to take out revenge on his enemy who had sworn to have David killed. David did not take revenge and stated how could he harm the anointed of God?

With this verse we clearly have bringing to our heart and spirit the commands of Jesus in that we should love not only our neighbors, but our enemies and we should pray for those who persecute us.

What a powerful and glorious church His bride would be today if we followed this command in its entirety. Indeed the world would certainly stand up and take notice that The Spirit of God was in us because we don't respond like the world. We love those who hate us and pray for those who persecute and use us.

Of course, David was not without his flaws. This is evidenced as he was up on the rooftop of his palace and he saw a woman bathing herself. The woman's name was Bathsheba. She was married to a soldier by the name of Uriah. David's carnal flesh was overcome with lust and he sent for the woman Bathsheba and he slept with her. Following this illicit sexual encounter, Bathsheba sent word to David that she was pregnant. Consequently they had a dilemma. How could Bathsheba be pregnant when her husband was off to war?

So David began to scheme and connive and sent for Uriah so that he could return home and eventually sleep with his wife. This plan would provide a cover-up reason on how Bathsheba had become pregnant. This plan of action would leave no one doubting that the baby was the child of Uriah and Bathsheba.

Conversely, Uriah was an honorable man and he chose not to sleep with his wife for he said how can I sleep with my wife when my men are still at war and their lives are in danger. Therefore, Uriah did not sleep with his wife Bathsheba.

David then conceived another plan and gave an order that Uriah be sent to the front lines so that he could be put in greater harm's way. This plan seemingly worked and Uriah was killed. David then legally took Bathsheba into his home to cover up their sin.

Remember though, God is not blind and always requires judgment and justice. He is not mocked. He sent unto David His prophet by the name of Nathan. Nathan in II Samuel 12:4 shares a story with David and asked what he would do with a man who took the only female lamb who belonged to a poor man and gave it to a rich man who had many female lambs? David got angry and said that the person who did this deserved to die. Then the spokesperson for the Lord, Nathan, said to David you are that man!

As we can see, even though David was a man after God's own heart, he still had human flaws that he gave into and created great wickedness by indulging in his fleshly desires. The man after God's own heart committed adultery and murder. This is obviously not an excuse for us to indulge in such behaviors, but shows God's wonderful grace and mercy to David and to all.

However, justice must be served!

In this matter, David is very much like Saul. Unlike Saul though, David repented and said to God against thee and thee only have I sinned. The question can be fairly asked that if both men, chosen of God, sinned, but only David, it appears, was restored why was not the same grace of God present in both men's lives.?

Perhaps a possible explanation of the two different paths following their disobedience can be explained in that God has given us free will. He does not force our obedience. He does not force our repentance. He does not force our brokenness of spirit. Therefore, it seems that David's relationship with God was restored through the forgiveness of sin whereas Saul's relationship was not restored because Saul's heart continually hardened following each episode of disobedience.

Gideon

Judges 6:34 (NIV) reads, "The spirit of the Lord came upon Gideon, and he blew a trumpet, summoning the Abiezerites."

Another mighty man of valor and hero of the faith is a warrior/leader called Gideon. Gideon, too, was anointed by The Holy Spirit and as such we see that he had a number of noble qualities as well. Those qualities include the fact that he is characterized by his humility (Judges 6:15), his spirituality (Judges 6:24), obedience (Judges 6:27), his loyalty to God (Judges 8:22, 23), etc.

The backdrop, for the nation of Israel, is seen in Judges 6:1 (NIV). This verse shares with us that "Again the Israelites did evil in the eyes of the Lord and for seven years he gave them into the hands of the Midianites." Consequently, we see that Gideon was anointed by God to be a light set on a hill amongst a dark nation. He was to show forth a commitment to God that was not exhibited in the land at the time.

It is also important to note that God still listens to His people and gives great grace. This is due to the fact that when the Israelite nation became repentant and cried out to God, God once again gave them a leader to restore His glory back to His people for His namesake. Is not this the pure definition of revival? Remember II Chronicles 7:14 (KJV), "If my people, which are called by my name, shall humble themselves and pray, and seek my face, and turn from their wicked ways; then will I hear from heaven, and will forgive their sin and will heal their land."

Of particular interest, when it comes to the life of Gideon, we see the beauty of God's power and grace as He responds to our low self-esteem and where we think we are at in regards to being used by God. In chapter 6 of Judges verse 15 (NIV), Gideon says the following, "But Lord, Gideon asked, how can I save Israel? My clan is the weakest of Manasseh and I am the least in my family."

Can we identify with Gideon in that he had a low self image?

Firstly, he says that his family itself is the weakest in all the land. How could he possibly serve the Lord? How could he possibly be used as a glorious vessel for His honor and glory? How could the weakness of the clan to which he belonged bring about the strength and power of God in restoration?

And not only does he say that his family is the weakest, but he goes on to say that I am least in my family. In other words Gideon is saying within the lowest family in the area I am the lowest of my family. Therefore he is saying I am the lowest of the low.

However, glory to His name, God answered positively. Again it would not be through Gideon's strength but through The Lord's strength as God says in verse 16 (NIV), "The Lord answered, "I will be with you and you will strike down the Midianites as if they were but one man."

It is then that Gideon asks for a sign and the familiar and famous Gideon's fleece is portrayed.

In the life of Gideon it is important to note that he did not feel qualified. However, God worked through the feelings of his inadequacies as God did and does with all men and women who are called by Him. When we are called of God He does not excuse our excuses. In fact, God truly chooses the lowly of life so that the works and accomplishments that are successfully performed are attributed to God and Him alone.

It appears from a brief study of the life of Gideon that the only weakness that Gideon demonstrates, other than his low self-esteem, is his desire for riches.

Some commentators attribute this weakness to the love for prosperity as seen in Judges 8:24 through 31. In these verses we see that Gideon asks of the people who plundered the Midianites the sharing of one earring from their share of the plunder that was gathered from this defeated nation.

Perhaps a take away from this possible flaw is that God should be our reward.

Elijah

In addition to these judges and kings and warriors that were utilized by God when His Spirit came upon them there are types of men known as prophets.

The interesting narrative about Elijah is that he bursts in on the scene without any introductions, no mention of his genealogy, no mention of his calling, nothing. Our introduction to him is found in I Kings 17:1. From this verse we notice that he is a Tishbite and is from the area known as Gilead. However, that appears to be all that we know about him.

Except for one magnificent thing!

He enters into the presence of King Ahab and as the Lord's spoke person, declares one profound, deep and powerful prophecy. He says in I Kings 17:1 (NIV), "As the Lord, the God of Israel, lives, whom I serve, there will be neither dew nor rain in the next five years except at my word."

From this verse, from this dynamic word of The Lord for us, our hearts are stirred as we see that The One whom Elijah represents is The Lord God of Israel. He is the ONE! He is The God of Israel! HE LIVES!

Elijah then goes on to say that it is the One God that Elijah serves. There are many things that can be taken away from this verse and fill our very being.

First of all, Elijah serves this One God. There is none other. There is no other motivation. There is no other master! And my desire and indeed my life, says Elijah, is all about service to Him.

From the palace of the King he is sent to the wilderness to be sustained by the ravens that God sends to him. They provide food to Elijah (God provides - Jehovah Jireh!) His ministry also takes him to the widow at Zarephath where, because of the drought, there is no food, but the miracle that God performs is for the jar of flour and oil to never run dry. (Could we use this as a reference today for the believer to realize that the bread of life and the oil of The Holy Spirit will never run out in our lives?). Elijah, through The Spirit of God also is used as a vessel to revive the widow's only son.

Elijah is a wonderful study of the ups and downs and greatness and flaws of mankind. This is seen as he enters the hall of the king of Israel and makes a declaration with boldness and courage and strength. From the king's palace he is then sent to the wilderness and then from the wilderness he is sent to the home of a widow and then from the home of the widow is sent again to the king's palace and then from the king's palace is sent to Mount Carmel and then from Mount Carmel he goes back to the wilderness. He is God's man whether it be in the palace of the king or whether it be on Mount Carmel battling with the false prophets of Baal.

However, despite the authority given to him by God and his prophesying, despite the miracle of sustenance in the wilderness through the ravens, despite the bringing back of the widow's son from the dead, despite the glorious response of God on Mount Carmel in answering by fire, Elijah becomes depressed.

It is interesting, as seen in chapter 19, that apparently Elijah becomes afraid because of Jezebel's, the wife of King Ahab, threat against Elijah. And so we see in Chapter 19 of I Kings verse 3 that Elijah was afraid and ran for his life.

Interesting that Elijah would so soon forget the victories and glory that God had used him to accomplish. But before we become so critical of Elijah, we need to realize that we probably have gone through the same things as well. It is so easy to take our eyes off of Jesus and place them upon the circumstances around us and consequently have our faith overshadowed by our doubt and disbelief.

However, Elijah is so distraught that he wishes for God to even take his life. In a conversation of self-pity he says to God that I've been very zealous for You, but the people have rejected Your covenant and broken down Your altars and put Your prophets to death with the sword and now I'm the only one left and their trying to kill me too. God did not answer him at that time, but said go up to a mountain and wait for my presence.

Then unfolds a magnificent and glorious event and a beautiful lesson that God is about to gift Elijah with. First of all a great wind came by and shattered the rocks, but God was not in the wind. Then there was an earthquake, but God was not in the earthquake. Finally came a fire and God was not in the fire.

But God did not want to demonstrate to Elijah, once again, what He could do through a demonstration of His power. He wanted to give Elijah a revelation about who He is; a lesson about His personality and the wonders of His presence in Elijah's life and ours.

And so God came in a whisper. It was a holy and glorious whisper which revealed God's heart, His persona and His loving care for those whom He created.

And He asked Elijah, "What are you doing here? Elijah then again went on his self-pity party and talked about the people not listening and God's prophets being killed and there was no one left but him.

God's response? Go on back and do and be what I've called you to do and be. He instructs Elijah to go and anoint Hazael as king over Aram. This command probably reminded of Elijah that he was God's prophet. A reminder of who he belonged to. A reminder that he was God's anointed and his ministry was to go and anoint those whom God had chosen. This again clarified the role and mission of Elijah and far more importantly who Elijah was in service to.

Finally, in I Kings 19:18 (NIV) God says to Elijah, "Yet I reserve seven thousand in Israel all whose knees have not bowed down to Baal and all whose mouths have not kissed him." In other words God is saying to Elijah, "Oh, and by the way Elijah you're not the only one. I still have left 7,000 individuals who are still faithful to me. They have not embraced idolatry. He graciously reminds Elijah that he is not alone in this. There are others that he doesn't know about.

Do we sometimes think we're alone and have become the Lone Ranger? We should ask God to open our eyes to see that others are faithful and are in the fight as well.

Deborah

In Judges 4:1 we see that once again, when a leader dies, the nature of the Israelite nation is again to turn their back on The Lord and do evil. Subsequently, God generally initiates some sort of punishment and in this case He gives the nation of Israel into the hands of the Canaanites.

The cycle continues for 20 years and we see that in verse 3 the Israelites again cry out to The Lord for redemption.

In this particular chapter, Judges 4, God does not send them a warrior nor does he send them a man. On this particular occasion he sends them a prophetess by the name of Deborah. Being a prophetess she most definitely has The Spirit of God upon her and she uses her gift from The Spirit to provide wisdom as she settles disputes amongst the nation of Israel.

In verse six she sends for a man by the name of Barak and says to him that he is to take 10,000 men and engage the army of Jabin. Barak listens, but says to Deborah I'm not going to go unless you go with me. Possibly Barak was afraid and needed the strength and courage that Deborah brought or perhaps recognized that Deborah was different because The Spirit of God was upon her and he needed to be emboldened by that presence.

In any case Deborah says to him very well then, but remember when the Army of Jabin has been defeated the honor will not be yours, but that The Lord will hand the victory over to a woman.

Consequently, in Judges 4:14 (NIV), we read of this command from Deborah to Barak saying, "Go! This is the day the Lord has given Sisera into your hands. Has not the Lord God gone ahead of you?" It is important to note that by the faith and the anointing of God in Deborah's life, we read of her great confidence in that the victory has already been won because God had led the way.

In conclusion, in highlighting the life of Deborah, chapter 5 of Judges records for us a song sung by Deborah and Barak. The song sings praises unto The Lord for His deliverance of the enemy into the hands of His people. Also, being the prophetess and anointed leader for God during this time, she rebukes those who did not engage in the battle.

Therefore, in the leader of Deborah we see a woman who is anointed of God and used mightily. She is endued with wisdom, insight, leadership skills, strength, courage (as seen in her willingness to go to battle), faith and faithfulness.

She is a woman of integrity and valor.

Chapter 5

Blazing Spiritual "Comets" Who Shook the Medieval Times

It has been the intent of this book to study The Holy Ghost. Specifically, our desire has been to show the generational workings of The Holy Spirit down through the ages.

In review, Chapter 3 was the stirring of The Holy Spirit in certain individual's lives before the coming of Christ and Chapter 4 highlighted the men and women of God who were used mightily by The Holy Spirit during the Iron Age.

Our journey now brings us to medieval times or the middle ages. This particular labeled age captures the 5th to the 15th century of recorded time.

With this chapter we will not only delve into the men and women of the early church as seen in the New Testament, but we will look outside of the New Testament. We will realize and discover that God The Holy Spirit was at work outside the recordings of the New Testament.

The Disciples

The first group of "comets" that we wish to be inspired by are the disciples of Christ. When we exclude Judas Iscariot, the betrayer, we have 11 disciples who for a period of three years walked with The Lord, observed His miracles, heard His teachings and were profoundly impacted by His life.

However, when Jesus was betrayed we see the humanness of each of the disciples, possibly with the exception of John the beloved, in that each scattered in various directions to escape persecution and in fear of their own lives. We read that even Peter, the rock, denied The Lord three times before the rooster crowed in the morning light.

We must make sure that we are not too harsh in our judgment of these disciples, for it seems like we would do the same thing. In fact, they had not received The Holy Spirit yet for Jesus had not yet been risen and ascended to the throne of The Father.

We also learn that following the crucifixion and death and burial of Jesus that like sheep they were all scattered and hid in fear that the Roman government would come after them and that they would realize the same fate as Jesus did. In fact on the Road to Emmaus, those that walked along that road probably echoed the sentiments of the disciples in that they said they thought that this was The Messiah, The One that would redeem Israel.

Therefore, following the passion of The Lord, the disciples were in disarray both personally and as followers of Jesus, they were afraid and in hiding in fear of their own lives and were in hiding behind locked doors (John 20:19).

But then we fast forward to Acts the 2nd chapter. What a difference when The Holy Spirit comes!

In this chapter we read that they were all together in one place. Suddenly the sound of a mighty rushing wind filled the whole house. Also revealed to us is that upon each of their heads, in that room, were tongues of fire that rested on each of them and that they were all filled with The Holy Spirit and began to speak in other languages as The Spirit enabled them.

This was Pentecost!

The Holy Spirit, The Promise of The Father, The Comforter, The Paraclete had come. And with The Holy Spirit's arrival, each of those in the upper room were transformed, empowered and were never the same again.

In fact, the crowd began to make fun of those saying that they've had too much wine. However Peter stood up and spoke boldly and confidently saying that we are not drunk, but this is what was spoken of by the prophet Joel that God would pour out His Spirit on all people.

Those in the upper room had become inflamed by the presence of The Holy Spirit they had truly become comets that radiated the light and power of God Almighty.

For us as believers, the message is clear, we each need to have our own personal Pentecost we need the filling of God The Holy Spirit, The Gift that God has given to us through the finished work of Jesus Christ. When The Holy Spirit comes we are transformed, the world takes notice, and the world that we enter into will never be the same.

In Acts 4:13 (KJV) people observed, "Now when they saw the boldness of Peter and John, and perceived that they were unlearned and ignorant men, they marveled; and they took knowledge of them, that they had been with Jesus."

These men and women were no longer afraid. They were no longer cowering in fear behind locked doors. Through Pentecost and the coming of The Holy Spirit, they were about to proclaim the gospel boldly, these vessels these men and women would be used of God to perform miracles and like men and women on fire they would and did ignite the world and spread the faith of Christianity to the whomsoever will may come.

As in the words of certain rulers in a city found in Acts 17:6 (KJV), "These that have turned the world upside down are come hither also;"

Stephen

It can be safely argued that the origins of Christianity were born from a violent beginning. This violence is not defined as wars, conflicts, or the use of weapons such as swords or spears.

No, the violent beginning of Christianity was the response of spiritual leaders to a message of love and grace and transformation from The loving God who sent his only begotten Son. The response of the powers of darkness to this message of love was the cross of Calvary and the crucifixion of the Son of God.

Of course, all of this was part of God's plan and for His will to be done.

Is it any wonder then that if The Leader, indeed The Christ of Christianity was treated in this manner, that his followers would be subject to the same potential violence. Jesus said in John 16:2 (KJV), "They shall put you out of the synagogues: yea, the time cometh, that whosoever killeth you will think that he doeth with God service."

Are there martyrs today? There most certainly are. All one needs to do is open up the newspaper and see the beheadings of Christians by terrorist groups because they simply stood for Christ.

In addition to physical martyrs, there are emotional martyrs in various families when family members have turned their backs upon those who have affirmed their faith in Christ. Or there are spiritual martyrs who choose to leave a sect or denomination that does not glorify The Christ.

Consequently, enter the first martyr whose name is Stephen.

In terms, for this study, Stephen was a flaming comet.

By way of introduction, we are first introduced to Stephen Acts 6:8 (KJV). We read, "And Stephen, full of faith and power, did great wonders and miracles among the people." From this verse, the Stephen that we are introduced to was first full of faith.

It is important to realize that faith is the primary prerequisite to a life of joy, power and fulfillment in our relationship with God through Jesus Christ our Lord. Indeed, in Hebrews 11:6 (KJV) we read, "But without faith it is impossible to please him: for he that cometh to God must believe that he is, and that he is a rewarder of them that diligently seek him." Faith is our foundation, our gateway to a relationship and deeper revelation of God by believing in the grace of our Lord Jesus Christ.

It is important to remember that it is by faith that we are saved (Ephesians 2:8, Galatians 3:26). Consequently, what greater attribute of Stephen is there to emulate in that he is described as being full of faith.

Building on his faith in Christ, we then see that he was full of power and did great wonders and miracles among the people. Did not our Lord say in John 14:12 (KJV) that we too would do great wonders and miracles? That verse reads "Verily, verily, I say unto you, he that believeth in me, the works that I do shall he do also; and greater works than these shall he do; because I go unto my father."

Additionally, Stephen was an anointed preacher.

At the end of Acts 6:15 (KJV), we read, "And all that sat in the council, looking steadfastly on him, saw his face as it had been the face of an angel." Stephen had been brought before the high priest and his counsel. There were accusations against Stephen regarding blasphemy against Moses and against God. In addition, there were false witnesses that lied about what Stephen was saying.

In Acts 6:15 (KJV), we, along with the others, are astounded as, "And all that sat in the Council, looking steadfastly on him, saw his face as it had been the face of an angel."

We are then led into the seventh chapter of Acts where Stephen is not about to back down and indeed is emboldened by The Holy Spirit as he begins his passionate message. Starting from the story of Moses to the deliverance of the Israelite nation from the bondage of Egypt through God's servant Moses to Solomon, Stephen gives the council both barrels of The Word of God.

The council's reaction was predictable as the Scripture says "They were cut to the heart" Acts 7:54 (KJV). And, as these rulers were filled with anger, The Scripture says that Stephen was filled with The Holy Ghost. The Scripture also shares that Stephen stated that he saw The Son of Man standing at the right hand of God (Acts 7:56).

Please note as well, that Stephen saw what no other person saw in that judgment room. He saw The Son of Man standing at the right hand of God. Notice, Jesus was standing, not sitting as seen in Colossians 3:1 (KJV) which states, "If ye then be risen with Christ, seek those things which are above, where Christ sitteth on the right hand of God."

It's almost as if Jesus, His Lord, was standing to welcome Stephen home. He would be there to greet His martyr and say, "Well done thou good and faithful servant: thou has been faithful over a few things, I will make thee ruler over many things: enter thou into the joy of thy lord" Matthew 25:21 (KJV). Also, the posture of Jesus almost denotes a respect and honor as when someone enters a room and people stand in their presence.

Additionally, in regards to spiritual vision, it is important to note that the person of God sees the reality of God rather than the reality of men. This spiritual vision is not only captured in Acts 7:56, but is also demonstrated in II Kings 6:16, 17 (KJV) when Elisha prayed that the servants eyes would be open, "And he answered, Fear not: for they that be with us are more than they that be with them. And Elisha prayed, and said, Lord, I pray thee, open his eyes, that he may see. And the Lord opened the eyes of the young man; and he saw: and, behold, the mountain was full of horses and chariots of fire round about Elisha."

We as believers should pray that the scales be removed from our eyes so that we may see as God sees.

Unable to bear the truth any longer, those who stood in judgment grabbed Stephen and carried him to a place outside of the city. It was there that they stoned him to death.

But, please hear and be saturated with the words of Stephen as they threw stone after stone at Stephen. In Acts 7:59, 60 (KJV) Stephen lovingly proclaimed, "And they stoned Stephen, calling upon God, and saying, Lord Jesus, receive my spirit. And he kneeled down, and cried with a loud voice, Lord lay not this sin to their charge. And when he had said this, he fell asleep."

Stephen, the first martyr of the Christian church was stoned to death for his belief, for his commitment, for his testimony, for his love of Jesus Christ, The Son of God. Being filled with The Holy Spirit, he prayed to God The Father to, in essence, forgive those who were murdering him and to not lay this sin upon their soul.

Additionally, why did this happen? What purpose did the martyrdom of Stephen serve? Why did this happen?

In Acts 7:58 (KJV) we read, "And cast him out of the city, and stoned him: and the witnesses laid down their clothes at a young man's feet, whose name was Saul."

Saul/Paul

Our first introduction to Saul is found in Acts 7:58. His story begins, as found in Acts 8:1 (KJV), where we read, "And Saul was consenting unto his death. And at that time there was a great persecution against the church..."

Following the martyrdom of Stephen we further read in verse 3, "As for Saul, he made havock of the church, entering into every house, and haling men and women committed them to prison."

If we briefly go back to the martyrdom of Stephen and ask the question of why, it is important to know that following Stephen's death the persecution of the church began. Consequently, because of this persecution, the church began to scatter throughout Judea and Samaria (Acts 8:1). Therefore, it is important to note that if God did not allow the death of Stephen and the subsequent persecution then the church would not have been scattered. Therefore, the message of Christianity would not have spread as it did.

The story of Saul, arguably the greatest comet that was utilized by God The Holy Spirit in the Christian church is a tremendous story of conversion.

Firstly, Saul's conversion is personal. We are probably well-versed in his conversion story as we recall he was traveling on the road to Damascus and had an encounter with The Living Christ. He was blinded by the intensity of that light and as he fell to the ground a voice asked, "Saul, Saul, why do you persecute me?" (Acts 9:4 NIV). Paul asked who are you and Jesus says I am the one that you are persecuting.

As probably has been pointed out to you the reader before, it is once again important to be reminded that when Jesus says He is being persecuted, He means that what is being done to His Church, The Bride, is also being done to Him.

Subsequently, Saul goes to the house of Judas on straight street and meets up with Ananias who then lays hands on "brother Saul" and the scales fell from Saul's eyes and he was filled with The Holy Spirit. It is also important to note in this sequence of events, depending upon your theology, that it seems that Saul had a conversion experience with the meeting of Jesus on the road to Damascus and then was filled with The Holy Spirit when Ananias laid hands on Saul. Saul then received baptism.

So, this is the personal and life transforming conversion of Saul. Another aspect of that personal conversion is seen in Acts 13:9 where Saul's name is changed to Paul. It is important to note that name changes in The Scripture are commonplace when there is a powerful spiritual event that takes place. Examples would be the name change of Abram to Abraham, Jacob to Israel, Sarai to Sarah, etc.

One possible explanation of Saul's name change to Paul is that Saul is his name in Hebrew and Paul would be his Roman name. Perhaps this name change is an indicator of the fact that he will become God's apostle to bring the Good News to the Roman Empire.

Another aspect to Paul's conversion is his religious perspective as seen in Philippians 3:4-10. In these verses, Paul gives us a tremendous insight into his religious beliefs. First of all he talks about being from the tribe of Benjamin and says that he is a Hebrew of the Hebrews. Additionally, when it comes to keeping the law he was a Pharisee (a Pharisee was known for keeping the religious law to the nth degree). He also addresses his zeal for his religion and how he persecuted the church mercilessly.

However, when he had an encounter with Jesus Christ, Who is the fulfillment of the law and our High Priest, he came away with a different perspective that shattered all of his beliefs. He truly had a religious, no spiritual experience. This is seen in the fact that he says those things that I thought were worth something, are in actuality nothing and I count them as loss to receive the fullness of Christ. In fact he goes on to say that I count everything as garbage so that I may win Christ. He then finishes up his testimony on his religious conversion by saying in Philippians 3:10 (KJV), "That

I may know him, and the power of his resurrection, and the fellowship of his sufferings, being made conformable unto his death;"

So, in order for a person to be fully utilized by God, that person must be fully surrendered to God. This is what we see in the conversion of Paul.

So, what made Paul, the great servant of God, so wonderfully used by The Holy Spirit to spread the gospel of Jesus Christ?

Was it the miracles he performed? In regards to Paul, God performed 7 miracles through His servant Paul. They are found in Acts 13:11, Acts 14:10, Acts 19:11-12, Acts 20:10-12, Acts 28:5 and Acts 28:8. These miracles range from causing someone to become blind, casting out an evil spirit, extraordinary miracles performed from objects that touched his body and were laid on others, resurrecting a young boy, shaking off a poisonous snake and healing a sick man.

Was it the suffering he endured? He was shipwrecked, imprisoned, involved with riots (Ephesus), lashed and beaten with rods and stoned (II Corinthians 11:24-27).

Or was it because he, Paul, preached the gospel and did so through his life and his words?

Yes, it was all of this, but remember it is not about people.

It is not about one's pastor or teacher or favorite author. This is clarified in I Corinthians 3:4-9 (KJV), "For while one saith, I am of Paul; and another, I am of Apollos; are ye not carnal? Who then is Paul, and who is Apollos, but ministers by whom ye believed, even as the Lord gave to every man? I have planted, Apollos watered; but God gave the increase. So then neither is he that planteth any thing, neither he that watereth; but God that giveth the increase. Now he that planteth and he that watereth are one: and every man shall receive his own reward according to his own labour. For we are labourers together with God" ye are God's husbandry, ye are God's building."

Paul's words by The Holy Spirit are confirmed in God's call of Paul and his purpose as seen in Acts 9:15, 16 (KJV). There we read, "But the Lord said unto him, Go thy way: for he is a chosen vessel unto me, to bear my name before the Gentiles, and kings, and the children of Israel: For I will shew him how great things he must suffer for my name's sake."

Therefore, Paul was greatly and mightily used by God by God's grace.

However, it is important to remember that we are all called and called for a specific reason and purpose. We may water, we may plant, but we labor together with God.

Saint Francis of Assisi

We now wish to turn our attention to one of the early leaders of the church whose life is not captured in The Scriptures, but one individual whose life and work is reflected through other Christian historical documentation.

That individual that we wish to study and be inspired by is St. Francis of Assisi.

St. Francis of Assisi went from a life of debauchery to a committed and sacrificial lifestyle to Christ his Savior.

He was born in Umbria, Italy in 1181. His early years, through a variety of written accounts, characterize his young life in terms of severe drinking and partying. He came from a wealthy lifestyle and paid little attention to the pursuit of serious issues. Physically he was very attractive and his personality could be described as being well mannered and gentlemanly.

Eventually he became a military officer in the Italian army and went to war against the neighboring geographical area known as Perugia.

It is reported that the experience of war revolutionized his life in a negative manner. This was due to the nature of war and Francis experiencing the brutality of armed conflict that left countless men dead and dying on the battlefield and those survivors mutilated by the atrocities of the weapons of the day.

It was during this time that he was captured by the enemy and held for ransom. Evidently, the enemy recognized that he was a man of wealth and that his parent's wealth invested in the best upbringing that money could buy. While he was in captivity he suffered physically and was inflicted with an illness that remained long after his release from his being captured.

It is important to pause at this moment in time to dwell upon our life's experiences and how they may impact our future. For St. Francis of Assisi perhaps, while in jail, he dwelt upon his extravagant lifestyle up to this point in time. Perhaps he meditated on the wastes that he had indulged in and God used this time of solitude to speak to his heart and convict him of his sins. Perhaps, he relived the horrors of the battlefield and dwelt upon the sorrow and suffering that those men had experienced. Or, just maybe, he wondered why his life was spared, for what reason and then possibly the question arose within him on how he was to spend his remaining years?

Subsequently, he rejoined the military to fight in the southern part of Italy. It was there that he came across a beggar. Evidently this beggar he recognized as a former and glorious military officer. As the story unfolds in this instance, St. Francis eventually gave, because he was greatly moved, his own quality clothing to the man.

Once again, St. Francis became ill and it was during this time that he began to experience various visions and unexplained activities of a mystical nature. It was after these episodes of mysterious accounts that St. Francis then went back to his home and started caring for those who were impoverished and in pain. It is said that these various visions were from God and that Francis, in response to the voice of Christ, began on a spiritual mission to help others and be part of the healing process of the Christian church. Biographers also mention that St. Francis felt he was called to live a life of poverty.

Consequently, he turned his back on his luxurious lifestyle and abdicated his wealth. His only focus became his faith and his efforts dedicated to spreading the Gospel.

His now peaceful demeanor and conversion to Christ and the love of God dwelling within him became his persona and character.

In closing our thoughts and lessons to be learned from the life of St. Francis of Assisi, we wish to conclude with the famous narrative regarding St. Francis and his encounter with a leper.

The story unfolds with St. Francis riding on his horse and he meets a leper. It is shared with us that St. Francis, looking down upon the leper, viewed the leper as Jesus himself (Hebrews 13:2, Matthew

25:40, 45). St. Francis dismounted and went over to the leper and hugged and kissed the man who was riddled with leprosy. It is recorded that St. Francis himself said that "The kiss that he placed upon the leprous man was like sweetness in his mouth."

In closing, the selection of St. Francis of Assisi as a blazing comet during medieval times was chosen for a number of reasons.

One of those reasons is because of his practical devotion to Christ our Lord. This practical devotion is not only seen in his declared vow of poverty, not for everyone of course, but the fact that his vow was made to Christ to help in rebuilding the church. Nothing else, materially or otherwise, would interfere with his focus.

In addition, his practicality of love and devotion is seen in his interaction, his loving interaction, with the leper. Truly this act of devotion and loving kindness could only be empowered by the work of The Holy Spirit in an individual.

Another reason why St. Francis Assisi is chosen is because he represents a sect of the Catholic Church known as the Franciscans. So often, based on a number of reasons and different theologies, we discredit other faiths and beliefs. However, we need to allow the words of our Lord Jesus, to bring to our hearts once more what he said in Luke 9:49,50 (KJV) with this instruction, "And John answered and said Master, we saw one casting out devils in thy name; and we forbade him, because he followeth not with us. And

Jesus said to him, forbid him not: for he that is not against us is for us."

Phebe

Our last comet during this time known as the medieval era that we wish to learn from is Phebe.

The only time that Phebe is mentioned in The Scripture is found in Romans 16:1 (KJV). In this verse we read, "I commend unto you Phebe our sister, which is a servant of the church which is at Cenchrea:"

So, what do we know about this sister in the faith?

We see that Paul commends her. The word commend here in this verse in the Greek language literally means to "set together", "to introduce", "to stand near", "approve", "command" or to stand (with).

With this word commend we see that Paul is vouching for her and he is endorsing her as a true servant of the church.

This is truly a powerful endorsement by Paul to the church at Rome. Behind this endorsement is the full spirituality and experience of Paul as a representative of Christ. It is an endorsement that does not come lightly and the practical application to us would be the question of whether we have ever received such an endorsement from such a powerful figure?

Indeed we have, as seen in John 16:23 (KJV), "And in that day ye shall ask me nothing. Verily, verily, I say unto you, Whatsoever ye shall ask the father in my name, he will give it to you." Yes, we have the endorsement of Jesus Christ Himself through our union with Him and therefore, access to The Father. We are commended by Christ.

Secondly, Paul refers to her as our sister. It is important to emphasize once again that being a Christian places us into the family of believers. We become brothers and sisters in Christ and indeed Christ is our Brother. Remember that in belonging to this family we are not alone and have a wonderful support system and we may ask others for practical help as well as prayers.

Notice also, that Paul calls her a servant. This word, *diakonon*, literally means, in the Greek language, "attendant, a waiter, and specifically in this context a deacon or deaconess.

It is important to note that we are servants. We are here, by His grace to serve one another. That servanthood is a mantle that humbly adorns us and calls us to serve nonbelievers, believers and above all God The Father through Jesus Christ The Son. Remember in Mark 9:35 (KJV), "And he sat down and called the twelve, and said unto them, If any man desire to be first the same shall be last of all, and servant of all."

Also remember that Jesus took up the towel of servanthood as seen in John 13:5 (KJV), "After that he poured water into a basin, and began to wash the disciples' feet, and wiped them with the towel wherewith he was girded." Remember, Jesus is the servant of all, not only did He wash the feet of the disciples in that upper room, but also washed the feet of the one who was to betray Him.

For those individuals who would minimize the role of women in the church, it is important to bring to those individual's attention sister Phebe.

The word "servant" here can also be translated from the Greek to mean deacon or deaconess. Therefore, Phebe was a spiritually gifted leader of the church. Her role could have been as an instrumental leader to both men and women, but most certainly was to women. She may have been officially anointed as a deacon, but she graciously accepted her role as servant and if that role relegated her to the service of delivering the manuscript or the letter or serving other people; she did it gladly as unto The Lord.

Finally, in verse 2 of Romans 16, Paul uses the word "succourer" to describe her service to him and many others.

This word, in the Greek, is *prostatis*. It literally means patroness or assistant and gives the visual of one who is standing by if needed.

One commentator associates the word with a trainer in the Olympic Games who assists the athletes in their training process.

Spectacular! What a ministry to brag about if one was to brag. Imagine standing by the "athlete" Paul to assist him in his race to win the prize. This exhortation to run is seen in I Corinthians 9:24 (KJV), "Know ye not that they which run in a race run all, but one receiveth the prize? So run, that ye may obtain."

And Phebe was Paul's assistant to his race as well as her own.

Remember, we are one body with many parts, but still one body.

Let us reclaim our spiritual role in this world as the Body of Christ by helping each other, ministering to each other and cheering each other on.

Chapter 6
The Great Awakening of Modern Era

In Mark 16:15 (KJV), we have recorded for us The Great Commission. In that verse we read the command of Jesus, "And he said unto them, go ye into all the world, and preach the gospel to every creature."

For each one of us as Christians, we have been given a mandate. That mandate is to go! We are not commanded to sit nor are we commanded to stay. As soldiers of Jesus Christ we have our marching orders and they are for each and every Christian. That command is to go and tell others the Good News, the gospel of Jesus Christ.

Through the Scriptures we see that God is always enlarging His tent. He is always reaching out to others through His love and shower upon those who are out of fellowship with Him His saving grace. If they will only accept His grace by faith.

Our study, for this chapter, continues to observe this progression of evangelism and revival of The Church of Jesus Christ.

His method of putting this plan into action and being successful is by mobilizing His church.

Therefore, in this chapter we continue to study the progression and work of God's church from the 16th century through to the 19th century. It is not possible, for the purpose of this study, to highlight every individual used by God during this time frame. Consequently, we have selected one individual that was mightily used by God to reach out to others in a particular point of time, for a particular purpose and within a particular geographical area.

Martin Luther

The introduction of Martin Luther begins with the state of the Roman Catholic Church at this time.

The Roman Catholic Church had become spiritually corrupt. This corruptness was first evidenced as The Word of God, which is the final word for spiritual instruction and religious teaching, no longer held that supreme place in the Roman Catholic Church. Indeed, the church officials and specifically the Pope had proclaimed themselves as the ultimate authority and thus replacing, in their mind and hearts, the authority of God's Word. Additionally, they imposed the same instruction upon the followers within the church.

Furthermore, the Catholic Church had become so corrupt that they began to try to sell salvation through the giving of money by the sinner. They unfortunately began granting "indulgences" for certain sins if, of course, the price was right.

An example of "selling salvation" to individuals to clear their conscience was evidenced by Friar Johann Tetzel in 1517. It is recorded for us that he began to sell these "indulgences" in Germany so that money could be raised in order to remodel St. Peter's Basilica in Rome.

Consequently, behind this backdrop of heresy in the church, God raised up a man. That man's name was Martin Luther.

Martin Luther was born in the year 1483 A.D. His birthplace was Eisleben, Saxony. This area is now modern-day Germany. He died in 1546 A.D.

Being brought up by wealthy parents he was able to enjoy a quality education. Additionally, at the age of 13 he began to attend a Catholic school. It was here that he began to be drawn to a monastic lifestyle.

Although Martin Luther had an interest in monasticism, his father had other plans for his son. In fact his father wanted him to become a lawyer and his son was withdrawn from the Catholic school and was soon enrolled in the prestigious University of Erfurt in Germany. He eventually obtained his Masters degree.

As his story unfolds, it is shared with us that in 1505, during the month of July, Martin Luther was caught in a very severe thunderstorm. It is further conveyed to us that a lightning bolt almost caused his demise. Given his Catholic teaching and early calling to be a monk, he saw and took this as a sign from God and made a vow to God. That vow was that if he survived the storm he would become a monk.

True to his word, he began to live the monastic lifestyle, but still continued his studies at the University of Erfurt.

In the year 1512, following continual study of The Bible, Luther's heart began to stir as, through God's Word, he began to obtain spiritual insight through the working of God, The Holy Spirit. Specifically, actions that were being taken by church that was contrary to God's Word.

On October 31, 1517, following the selling of indulgences by Friar Johann Tetzel of the same year, Martin Luther wrote to his bishop. The bishop's name was Albert of Mainz.

In that letter he referenced the selling of indulgences and strongly protested against that non-Biblical act of church forgiveness. That letter was entitled "Disputation of Martin Luther on the Power and Efficacy of Indulgences.

It later became known as the 95 Theses. One of the questions posed in this writing asked why the did the money of the poor build the Basilica of St. Peter when the Pope actually had significant wealth that he could use from his own coffers?

When these Ninety-five Theses were nailed to the door of the all Saints Church in Wittenberg, all though this account is disputed, it became fuel to ignite the fire that spread from Germany and throughout Europe and eventually into England.

The emphasis of the doctrine and reality of justification by faith alone again became the central belief of forgiveness of sin through God's grace. Through Luther's "protest" began the movement known as Protestantism in response to the departure of the Roman Catholic Church. In their corruptness, Catholic leadership was stating that spiritual salvation could be paid for rather than the repentant coming to God though faith and receiving salvation by grace through faith.

It is also recorded, that Martin Luther quoted Matthew 16:18 and boldly asserted that the Pope did not have the ultimate right to translate Scripture and as a consequence neither the Pope nor any of the church councils were the ultimate authority on God's Word.

That verse in the King James Version reads, "And I say also unto thee, that thou art Peter, and upon this rock I will build my church; and the gates of hell shall not prevail against it."

Of course the Roman Catholic Church fought back against Martin Luther. He was labeled a heretic and was summoned by Rome on the hopes that he would recant his words against the Catholic Church.

Needless to say, Luther soon found himself excommunicated from the church. The Pope at this time was Pope Leo X.

During the 16th century, God needed a person to stand heart to hardened heart with the Catholic Church that was preaching heresy. The church was leading many astray and was betraying The Son of God and His sacrifice at Calvary by proclaiming that man could purchase his salvation when in fact Jesus Christ purchased our salvation. This salvation is available to all through grace by faith.

God found his person in Martin Luther.

The spiritual insight for us is that first of all, even though his earthly father wanted him to study law and become a lawyer, God, his Heavenly Father had other plans. With God's hand upon him, rather than becoming an attorney through the study of law he became a agitator, a protester who proclaimed the grace of Christ, who is the fulfillment of the law.

Additionally, we can not underestimate the power of God's Word. Luther was a student of The Word and The Word, hidden in Luther's heart, allowed him to be courageous as he boldly spoke the truth and confronted the religious leaders of the day including standing up to the very pope.

Also, when it comes to God's calling, God can speak to us in a variety of ways and utilize a number of methods. God spoke to Moses through a burning bush. He can speak through a blinding light as He did with Saul/Paul. He also spoke to Balaam through Balaam's donkey. For Martin Luther, he encountered a thunder storm and made a vow. God took him at his word.

One other lesson that we can learn from our brief study of Martin Luther is to recognize the traps that can occur when religion and religious leaders compromise The Truth. The Scripture cautions us and truthfully declares that, "For the love of money is the root of all evil:" (I Timothy 6:10 KJV).

Another significant trap is lust as seen in the life of David or the sin of pride. These sins are underscored in I John 2:16 (KJV), "For all that is in the world, the lust of the flesh, and the lust of the eyes, and the pride of life, is not of the Father, but is of the world."

When the church or church leaders go down these paths of sin, often God calls upon the Body of Christ or individuals to confront that sin which is in the camp. Luther confronted the church. The church did not repent and consequently, the church needed to be purged. This purging resulted in a breaking away from the Roman Catholic Church and restoring The Church with purity, power and glory as the Bride of Christ.

John Bunyan

It has been correctly said by George Santayana that "Those who do not learn from history are doomed to repeat it."

Dove tailing on the reformation involving the protest against the Roman Catholic Church, the Christian revival moved from Europe to England. Under the reign of King Henry VIII there was a repudiation of the Pope's authority and subsequently, the Roman Catholic Church transformed into the Church of England. However, the Church of England maintained much of the thoughts and beliefs of the Roman Catholic Church and indulged in the liturgy and ritualism of Catholicism.

Therefore, there were many within the Protestant movement that maintained that the reformation movement had not gone far enough.

Consequently, out of the Church of England came a further division or breaking away from the beliefs and rituals followed by the Church of England.

This new movement became known as Puritanism. Additionally, because of this movement being defined as rebellious, they were persecuted to the point of either being exiled or sent to their death.

The Puritans were known for their strict reliance and obedience to the Word of God. They often were ridiculed for their lifestyle and often called hypocrites because of their beliefs conflicting with their actions.

However, God used this group of believers as witnessed through their fleeing from persecution to the New World and specifically Plymouth, New England.

One specific Puritan that we wish to learn from and be inspired by through the work of The Holy Spirit within him is the Puritan known as John Bunyan.

John Bunyan was born in the early 1600's and was an English writer and Puritan preacher. After a three-year stint in the Army he returned to his home village of Elstow in England. It is this experience, during the course of his military experience, that he learned the language associated with being in the Army and would eventually use this language in illustrations in his writings.

Bunyan's trade was that of a tinker as that was the occupation of his father. A tinker is a craftsman that works with and repairs metal objects.

After serving in the military he married. He and his wife had four children and the oldest daughter was born blind. Unfortunately in 1658 Bunyan's wife died leaving him as the sole parent of the four children. He did, however, remarry one year later.

Following the restoring of the monarchy to the throne in England, Puritan preachers were no longer allowed to preach. This did not stop John Bunyan from fulfilling his calling to preach the word in season and out. He was arrested and sentenced to jail for three months. He was also told that he would be released at the end of that imprisonment if he agreed not to attend the parish church and if he would stop preaching.

It is also important to note that Bunyan was given, by The Holy Spirit, the gift of preaching/teaching/exhortation. It is recorded for us that his unction from The Holy Spirit stirred people's hearts to hear The Word of God. In fact, hundreds would come to hear him expound on God's Word. Additionally, they came from all over the countryside and at strange hours such as 7:00 a.m. on a weekday.

One personal account from a man by the name of Charles Doe shares that, "Mr. Bunyan preached no New Testament - like he made me admire and weep for joy, and give him my affections."

One of John Bunyan's contemporaries said of his preaching, "I would willingly exchange my learning for the tinker's power of touching men's hearts."

However, he refused the order to stop preaching and subsequently was incarcerated for a total of 12 years. Despite the hardship that this brought upon his wife and family of four, he chose to obey God. He is quoted as saying, "Oh I saw in this condition I was a man who's pulling down his house upon the head of his wife and children; yet but I must do it, I must do it."

While in prison this writer and preacher had two books in his possession. One was his copy of the Bible and another was John Fox's *Book of Martyrs*.

After his release in 1672, Bunyan obtained a certificate of license to preach the gospel.

What makes John Bunyan's life a shining light, inspiration to Christians and an example of being used by God The Holy Spirit, is the fact that during his imprisonment he wrote one of the classic Christian books that was and is widely read.

That book is Pilgrim's Progress. This book is an allegory depicting the Christian's spiritual journey to The Celestial City. The hero's name, in the book, is Christian and he lives in the City of Destruction. He reads a book that talks about his and his family's impending judgment. After meeting another man by the name of Evangelist, Christian decides to take the narrow path that leads to The Celestial City. He reaches a hill where stands a cross and there his burden, that he has been carrying, rolls downhill. However, his journey does not end there and, as a pilgrim, he encounters a series of challenging situations and meetings with other pilgrims. Christian eventually reaches his destination.

The life of John Bunyan is an inspiration to believers today.

An inspiration because he was obedient to God's call for him to preach the gospel. He did not waiver from God's calling in his life. In fact, this was no easy matter for him to be obedient to God and came at great sacrifice. This is due to the fact that he basically chose God's calling over his family and lost his family for 12 years because of his obedience to God and his commitment to preach the word. His obedience extended a three month jail term to 12 years.

Many would question why Bunyan didn't simply denounce his role as a preacher so that his jail time would have only been three months rather that 12 years. They would argue that he was not a good provider for his family.

However, does not God's Word say in Matthew 10:37 (KJV), "He that loveth father or mother more than me is not worthy of me: and he that loveth son or daughter more that me is not worthy of me."

Along with John Bunyan, we as Christians should take to heart the words of Peter and John as seen in Acts 4:18 -20 (KJV), "And they called them, and commanded them not to speak at all nor teach in the name of Jesus. But Peter and John answered and said unto them, Whether it be right in the sight of God to hearken unto you more than unto God, judge ye. For we cannot but speak the things which we have seen and heard."

Another spiritual lesson that we can gather from this preacher is found in the words of Joseph. In Genesis 50:20 (KJV) we read, "But as for you, ye thought evil against me; but God meant it unto good, to bring to pass, as it is this day, to save much people alive."

The reality is that the seeming hardships of the world that come our way and are meant to minimize our effectiveness for Christ, are simply stepping stones for us that God uses to bring about greater glory for Him and His Church. This faithfulness and good from evil is witnessed even today through the writing of John Bunyan in his classic spiritual allegory of Pilgrim's Progress.

Additionally, John Bunyan was a true disciple of Jesus Christ as when he put his hand on the plow, he did not look back (Luke 9:62 - KJV). As a true disciple he took up the cross and followed Jesus as seen in Matthew 16:24 (KJV), "Then said Jesus unto his disciples, if any man will come after me, let him deny himself, and take up his cross, and follow me."

Jonathan Edwards

We now travel across the Atlantic Ocean from England and Europe to America.

One such Puritan preacher for colonial America was Jonathan Edwards. He was an integral part of God's plan during what is known as the Great Awakening.

Born in 1703 into a family of 11 children, he was the only son of Timothy and Esther Edwards. Both of his parents were considered educated people which provided Jonathan with a quality education. Edward's father was also a preacher and teacher.

As a young boy, Jonathan Edwards was an avid reader and writer. At the age of 14 he read Locke's writing on Human Understanding.

Edward would often record his musings and thoughts in notebooks which would find their way into future sermons that he delivered.

He attended Yale College at the age of 13 and graduated three years later.

Although brought up in a Christian home, Edwards didn't receive salvation by faith until he was about 20 years of age. He eventually became the pastor at the First Church of Northampton. He was devoted to feeding the flock of God by providing his congregation with passionate sermons that were born of detailed study over The Word of God.

Because he took to heart the words found in II Timothy 4:2 (KJV) , "Preach the word; be instant in season, out of season; reprove, review, exhort with all long-suffering and doctrine", a great awakening occurred in the minds and spirits of those who heard God's Word.

It is historically recorded that a great number, estimated to be in the hundreds, of individuals came to a saving knowledge of Jesus Christ. This revival or Great Awakening was unlike any that occurred either in the Americas or abroad.

One of his most powerful sermons was entitled "Sinners in the Hands of an Angry God." In this particular message to his congregation he talked about sinners being held "over the pit of hell much as one holds a spider, or some loathsome insect, over the fire."

It is recorded that as the sermon was being delivered, Edwards would be interrupted several times. Many people began to cry out and asked what they needed to do to be saved?

It is said that following the deliverance of this sermon that New England never forgave Jonathan Edwards. This is because the sermon was very controversial in nature. However, God The Holy Spirit used Jonathan Edwards and this message to fan into a flame a revival that began the Great Awakening.

Additionally, some of his sermons addressed God's sovereignty, the triune God, the free will of man and of course repentance from sin and the sinners need for a Savior.

Eventually, he was removed from the pulpit at Northampton. Following his dismissal he was offered the pastorate at a church in Stockbridge. It was there that he had the opportunity not only to minister to Caucasian parishioners but also spoke of salvation to the Native Americans.

At the age of 53, he died in 1758 while serving as the president of Princeton.

There is a warning issued by Paul, as seen in II Timothy 4:3 (KJV), that speaks of preaching that is not doctrinally sound. That verse reads, "For the time will come when they will not endure sound doctrine; but after their own lusts shall they heap to themselves teachers, having itching ears."

Jonathan Edwards was God's person, during God's perfect timing and delivered God's message. This message was not one of prosperity nor was it simply a message of come to God but don't worry about your lifestyle or the fact that you are a sinner. It was indeed a message of God's Love and the atoning work of His Son Jesus Christ to save people from the pit of hell.

And so, the message to us today, straight from the heart and lips of Jonathan Edwards, is to preach The Word. That preaching of The Word is sometimes not popular, but is the message unto salvation.

Additionally, some of the doctrines taught in The Word of God are sometimes watered down today or even ignored. As followers of Christ we must not only preach the full Gospel, but live the full Gospel as well and not be dissuaded. Christians and leaders in the Church are not called to win a popularity contest. They are called to be light and salt in a dark and spoiled world.

Another lesson that the life of Jonathan Edwards teaches us is that for a follower of Christ to start a fire in the life of other people, he or she must be on fire themselves to ignite others. We must have a burden for others and a vision of what God desires to do. This truly will make us a missionary.

Finally, we see that God's intercedes in our life and creates history. Perhaps, the Great Awakening was needed to not only bring Him glory and honor as people came to a saving knowledge of Christ, but perhaps this was part of God's timing to help usher in the United States of America; a country that was built on the premise of being one nation under God.

William Booth

As Christians we find ourselves in the world, but we are not to be of the world. This simply means that even though we live in this world, our citizenship is in heaven.

Therefore, as we travel or sojourn in this world we cannot help but be moved by God's Holy Spirit as it relates to others when we see their suffering, pain and being out of fellowship with Him.

Our study now takes us to 19th century England and specifically the City of London. The contrast between the haves and the have-nots was very stark. The rich lived lavish lifestyles and the poor provided for those lifestyles through their hard work and suffering.

Specifically, in 1865, if one wants to travel in the east part of London during this time they would be outraged. That is because every fifth house in this area of London was devoted to the selling of alcohol. In fact, there was no age limit as most taverns had specially made steps to serve even the youngest of customers. Indeed, one sign in a tavern proudly proclaimed "drunk for a penny and dead drunk for two.

Additionally, as one would imagine, various other social ills associated with the use of alcohol were rampant and blatantly on sale in this area of London.

This degenerate and egregious behavior was most certainly not lost on the heart of God and so he secured an individual to reach out to these particular individuals who were lost.

William Booth, General of The Salvation Army, was born in 1829 in an outlying area of Nottingham, England. His family was not religious and could be described as the working poor. He had little education and at the age of 14 his father died.

Around the age of 15, William booth attended a Wesleyan religious service and it was there that he was converted to a saving knowledge of Jesus Christ. He was to write later on, "God shall have all there is of William Booth."

Indeed, God heard that vow and took him at his word and Booth eventually became an evangelist to the poor.

He and a group of friends began to preach on the streets of East London. These services were known as open airs. Additionally, in order to attract the individuals from the bars he would put evangelistic words and messages to the bar room tunes. These tunes, accompanied by brass instruments, attracted those individuals and then William Booth would preach the gospel. For an altar of repentance and commitment they would lay down the big bass drum and many drunks came to a saving knowledge of Jesus Christ. Many criticized the use of secular music to proclaim the gospel, but William Booth said "Why should the Devil have all the good music."

The question then rose as to how to incorporate those that had been saved into a church so that they could be taught and their discipleship could mature. As one can imagine, these folks, because of their chosen lifestyle, were often dirty, disheveled and not pleasant to look at. Consequently, the "established" churches didn't want anything to do with these recent converts.

In fact, the Methodist Church, of which William Booth was a reverend, gave William Booth and his wife Catherine an ultimatum. That ultimatum was that they either give up this ministry or leave the Methodist Church. As Catherine Booth shouted from the rafters in the church the words, "never William never," the decision was made and William Booth then went on to begin the London Christian mission which eventually became The Salvation Army.

Today, as it was then, many criticized William Booth for proclaiming a social gospel. However, nothing could be further from the truth regarding the doctrine of William Booth's Salvation Army. He believed wholeheartedly in the cleansing power of the blood of The Lamb and, true to his Methodist background, believed in a life of holiness.

In fact, William booth is quoted as saying that in reaching out to the poor it was difficult to talk about eternal matters and a relationship with Christ when the individual was hungry and in need of being clean outwardly. He often used the phrase "Soup, soap and salvation."

When William Booth died, it is estimated that 150,000 people filed by his casket and 40,000 individuals attended his funeral. One of the attendees at his funeral included Queen Mary.

But, most importantly of all, we are sure that he met King Jesus and The King said to him "Well done thou good and faithful servant" (Matthew 25:21 KJV).

Today, it is next to impossible to walk down the streets of any city and not see the homeless. Often, we will toss them a few coins in hopes that they will leave us alone and that our conscience will be satisfied. However, it is important to realize that these individuals may be a brother, a sister, a mother, or a father to someone. They are human beings and they are part of that whosoever in the world that God so loves.

The lessons for us as we reflect on the life of General William Booth are that God stirred this man's heart to reach out to a lost segment of society. He was called to reach out to these individuals and share with them The Gospel, The Good News of Jesus Christ. His church was in the alleyways, outside the taverns and outside the brothels. He used everything within his means to glorify The Lord and bring others to a saving knowledge of Jesus Christ. His weapons were brass instruments, tambourines, secular tunes and uniforms. By faith he used everything he could to reach out to others who were lost.

He chose the term The Salvation Army because he knew that the Christian Church was at war with the evil one. The goal of this war is the most precious of all reasons to fight. The souls of men, women and children.

It is important also to note that William Booth went to where the sinner was. He went to their environment; he marched into the very depths of depravity through the power of The Holy Spirit. As soldiers of Christ we must take the offensive, we must go to the highways and byways. This is the fulfillment of the Great Commission.

The life of William Booth also reveals to us, through his vow as a teenager, that God shall have all there was of William Booth. Romans 12:1 (KJV) pleads, "I beseech you therefore, brethren, by the mercies of God, that ye present your bodies a living sacrifice, holy acceptable unto God, which is your reasonable service."

Chapter 7
These Signs Shall Follow Those Who Believe

In the New Testament, the phrase "signs and wonders" is used 14 times. However, it is used in a negative manner three times of these 14. In those three Scriptural references it refers to the actions of false Christs and false prophets (Matthew 24:24 and Mark 13:22) and in John 4:48 against those who need these demonstrations in order to believe.

The remaining verses that incorporate "signs and wonders" refer to these indicators of God's blessing as a witness of God's outpouring through The Presence of God The Holy Spirit in these situations.

A revival is defined as an improvement in the condition or strength of something. Revival can also be defined as an occurrence that makes something valuable or important again.

For the purposes of this non-exhaustive study, let us define revival in terms of a person who has stopped breathing and they are revived when some activity starts their breathing once more. This is physical revival and church revival is an outpouring of The Spirit of God breathing out His reviving breath and power.

Our study for this chapter takes us into the 20th century as we focus on men and women of God, chosen vessels, utilized by God to bring about conversions, Pentecost type outpourings of God The Holy Spirit and demonstrated with signs that followed on those that believe.

William Seymour

One of the most powerful and God glorifying revivals of recent modern times is the Azusa Street revival.

The geographical area in which this revival took place is located in Los Angeles, California.

One of the key figures utilized by God in ushering this revival forth was William Seymour.

William Seymour was born to former black slaves in the year 1870. The state of his birth was Louisiana. As a young child he was subjected to prejudices because of his being an African American. His education was limited and his biographers indicate that he experienced many visions of God.

His religious upbringing was varied. He was baptized as a Catholic, but also joined other religious denominations such as the Baptists and Methodists. Accordingly his belief system incorporated the various doctrines from these churches. Some of those doctrines included holiness and immediate sanctification of the believer. He also believed that the return of Christ was imminent and would be superseded by a miraculous acceptance of different races in worship.

He also suffered physically when he incurred the disease of small pox. This disease left him without sight in his left eye. This disease proved to be a catalyst for him becoming a preacher of The Gospel.

Following his ordination, as a minister within the Church of God, Seymour became an itinerant evangelist and eventually settled in Houston, Texas and temporarily replaced Lucy Farrow who ascribed to the doctrine of Holiness.

Leading up to and during this time, Seymour became very interested in *glossolalia* or speaking in tongues. Pastor Farrow told Seymour of a minister by the name of Parham who would eventually teach Seymour about this gift. However, Parham was a segregationist and would only allow Seymour to listen at the door or window.

Another person who had an influence on the life of Seymour was a woman by the name of Neely Terry. She was from the city of Los Angeles and embraced the teaching of holiness. Subsequently, for whatever reason, Seymour made his way out to Los Angeles and was invited to preach at a holiness church established by a woman named Julia Hutchins. True to his beliefs, Seymour exhorted the congregation regarding the importance of the various races accepting each other and the importance of speaking in tongues as a sign of one's baptism by The Holy Spirit. This teaching was met with mixed reviews and eventually Seymour was locked out of this church and prohibited from preaching.

This then led to an invitation of Seymour to be with Mr. and Mrs. Richard Asberry. The Asberrys held religious services out of their home on a street called North Bonnie Brae. Seymour continued preaching about racial unity and manifesting The Holy Spirit as evidenced by the gift of tongues.

On April 9, 1906 one particular spiritual meeting occurred and at that meeting there were signs that followed as the congregation met to worship The Lord. The signs and wonders at this gathering included reports of miraculous healings including the blind receiving their sight and illnesses being cured. Also, there was the uttering of languages being spoken such as German, Spanish and

Yiddish by non-educated African Americans with translation into English through supernatural means.

For three nights the zeal for The Lord was evidenced and then on April 12th, William Seymour himself spoke in tongues.

Additionally, in an era of segregation, no such separation took place at all, as it seems all were gathered in one accord (Acts 1:14). Through the outpouring of The Holy Spirit there are no differences in race and ethnicity as these differences are cast aside.

Subsequently, many individuals began to attend services and it was realized that a larger facility would need to be obtained. A new meeting place was acquired at 312 Azusa Street. The church name was the Apostolic Faith Mission. It is here that most generally acknowledge this locale as the birthplace of Pentecostalism.

It is reported that three services were conducted during the course of the day. It is also estimated that over one thousand people attended services every day. Eventually, this great revival, this Pentecostal Movement that was initiated and used by God, exploded into 20 million members in the United States and globally into 200 million members.

About a year later, the zeal of the movement began to wane and factions began to arise within. In 1911 a white preacher attempted to usurp Seymour, but the actions of that preacher failed.

Seymour's final days were still spent preaching The Word to mainly black believers. In the year 1922 on September the 28th, William Seymour died as a result of two heart attacks.

The Azusa Revival is credited with being the start of Pentecostalism and William Seymour as God's instrumental vessel to usher in this revival on the west coast.

The life of William Seymour is a burning testimony and inspiration to believers today in a number of ways.

First of all, it is important to note the many hardships that William Seymour faced. The obvious hardship was that he was African-American; a hardship not because of his color, but the attitude, prejudice and bias of others that he experienced. However, he endured, indeed overcame, the reality of discrimination in this world and would not allow misplaced legislation to keep him from learning and fulfilling his calling from God.

Also, he was the son of freed slaves. The mental stigma that could be associated with this label and the reality of those who sought to keep him in shackles was not embraced by William Seymour. Indeed, he found his freedom in Christ. This glorious affirmation is found in Galatians 3:28 (KJV) which states, "There is neither Jew nor Greek, there is neither bond nor free, there is neither male nor female: for ye are all one in Christ Jesus."

Another hardship that he endured was being stricken with the disease of smallpox. However, he embraced this disease as a sign from God in that he was spared his life and therefore he committed his energies to full-time service as a minister of The Lord and His gospel.

A further life lesson to learn from this minister of the gospel is that he himself did not practice prejudice. This is seen in the various encounters that he had with women within the ministry. In fact, the women that he spiritually associated with were greatly used of God to influence his life and open various doors to lead him to Azusa.

As equally important is for us to draw inspiration from his life of obedience. Despite the fact that he had multiple church affiliations, moved to various states within America, was locked out of churches and was betrayed by churches, he never lost sight of The One who called him. This speaks of his obedience, the carrying of the cross of Jesus and his confidence in his beliefs as revealed to him by God The Holy Spirit.

As an aside to the life of William Seymour it may be interesting to note that the great earthquake of San Francisco occurred on April 18, 1906. Perhaps this is a coincidence in regards to a physical earthquake happening during the same time the spiritual earthquake was happening in the same state.

Or perhaps, God utilizes the forces of nature or causes the forces of nature to gain the attention of His creation. Certainly, there had to be those individuals who did not lose sight of the fact that a catastrophic event had happened and perhaps God was speaking to those individuals in and through that catastrophe.

John G. Lake

John G Lake was born in 1870 in Ontario, Canada into a family of 17 brothers and sisters. He was well acquainted with death and sickness as eight of his siblings died when he was a young boy. He too was inflicted with rheumatism, but experienced God's healing through the ministry of John Alexander Dowrie's healing ministry in Chicago.

He was known as God's apostle to Africa. However his preparation journey prior to wearing this mantle as a missionary to Africa can be characterized as one of obedience, believing God and His word, hunger for the baptism of The Holy Spirit and spiritual patience.

His denomination of worship began with the Methodist Church and it was here that he soon began to believe wholly and solely in the healing power of God.

At the age of 23, Lake married a woman by the name of Jenny Stevens. Soon after their marriage she was diagnosed with tuberculosis and heart disease. Unfortunately Lake's wife died as a result of her afflictions and in an act of anger against God, Lake threw his Bible against a nearby fireplace.

When he went to pick up his Bible it laid open at the 10th chapter of Acts and his eyes were drawn to verse 38 which says, in the King James version, "How God anointed Jesus Christ with the Holy Ghost and with power: who went about doing good, and healing all that were oppressed of the devil; for God was with him."

Lake confessed that he was blaming God for his wife's illness when in fact it was the evil one's doing of creating evil in this world.

Lake further relates that his wife, medically, had died. However, he couldn't bear to think of his wife's passing and so he believed God that she would be delivered from death. It is verified that within the hour Jenny's life had been revived. In fact, the news of her miraculous recovery became well-known across the country which brought many to their home to witness firsthand the miracle wrought by God.

In addition to being thankful to God for His providential care, this further dedicated John Lake's resolve towards a deeper walk with The Lord and be more fully immersed in the baptism of The Holy Spirit.

The public ministry of John Lake began in 1888, but he realized that his ministry paled in comparison to the ministry as reflected in the Book of Acts. Consequently, his hunger for a greater baptism of the Holy Ghost grew and grew. In fact it wasn't till several years later that the "the experience" came to him.

Following an intense hunger for the fullness of God, Lake testifies that he had set aside certain hours within the day. He would use these hours strictly for meditation and prayer. It was during this time that he heard the voice of The Lord telling him to be patient. Lake went on to say that even though he was involved with the commonalities of the day, his spirit was in constant communion with The Spirit of God.

For nine months the supplication of Lake was to The Lord for His fullness. One time, while praying with other believers, he became aware of a light. He defined the light in terms of purity and being an extreme whiteness. As this occurred, he was painfully convicted of his transgressions. He further relates that these transgressions had remained hidden in the deepest and darkest recesses of his soul. God reached into those areas and purged and purified is being.

Then one day, the glory of The Lord descended upon John G. Lake. Lake testifies that he and a fellow minister were attending to the needs of a lady who was stricken with inflammatory rheumatism. As the brother was conversing with the woman, John says that his attention was given over to God and he shares that he was crying out with such a thirst. Suddenly, Lake states that he felt a "warm tropical rain, which was not falling upon me, but through me." He went on to say that his spirit felt such serenity that he had never known before and that even his brain had become so serene. He testifies that the presence of God settled over him.

Following his baptism in The Holy Spirit he could no longer concentrate on his successful business in the same committed way that made him so prosperous. In fact, when customers or potential customers came to his office his only concentration and focus of the meeting was their relationship with God through Jesus Christ.

Finally, he parallels his business journey with that found in Matthew 9:9 (KJV) when Jesus said to Matthew, "And as Jesus passed forth from thence, he saw a man, named Matthew, sitting at the receipt of custom: and he saith unto him, Follow me. And he arose, and followed him." As the Master had called Matthew from his business endeavors, so did he call John G. Lake and Lake closed the business, sold all of his assets, gave the money to charity and kept only one dollar.

He had become totally dependent upon the Lord for not only his physical needs, but his spiritual needs.

God's provision is further demonstrated as Lake arrived in South Africa in 1908. According to local law he needed to give the immigration Department a total amount of $125 for his entry into the country. Obviously he had no money, but his Father owns the cattle on thousand hills. He also believed that God would supply his every need according to his riches in glory by Christ Jesus as found in Philippians 4:19 (KJV). True to his word God provided through a man, who said that he didn't know Lake, but stated that he felt led to give him $200.

In addition, Lake did not have a place to stay along with his wife when they arrived in South Africa. While waiting at the train station another stranger came up to them. She stated that The Lord had sent her to offer him and his family a home, at no charge.

John G. Lake hungered for the fullness of God. He believed that the same church found in the Book of Acts was the same church that could glorify The Lord during his day. And so he pursued God and found in fact, that God was pursuing him to do great things in bringing about The Kingdom of God and glorify His Name.

Under the Ministry of John G. Lake, 1 million converts were brought to a saving knowledge of Jesus Christ along with the planting of 625 churches and the ordination of 1,250 preachers during his five years of ministry in South Africa.

In addition, upon returning to the United States, he settled in Spokane, Washington. It was there in the city that, under his ministry, 100,000 miraculous healings occurred.

The life and ministry of John G. Lake speaks volumes to our hearts.

First of all, God creates spiritual hunger within us that can only be satisfied by receiving the fullness of the Bread of Life, which is The Spirit of Christ. Lake's life also inspires our being about faith and his belief in God's Word to have a personal Pentecost. By faith he believed and it pleased God.

In addition, the world will be astounded when a man or a woman is given wholly over to The Holy God. Then truly, will we experience for ourselves, as well as the world being astounded, when the glory of God is revealed.

Please also note that the treasures of this life pale in comparison to the treasure we have in receiving The Pearl of Great Price (Matthew 13:46)." When Jesus comes in His fullness, this world and the things of this world are nothing.

Also, reflected in his biography, is the importance of us needing to be clean vessels in order for the Lord to fill His temple. In Psalm 139:23 (KJV), the psalmist cries out, "Search me, O God, and know my heart: try me, and know my thoughts:"

In order for the fullness of God's Spirit to fill His vessel, Lake's heart was purged to the very deepest and darkest recesses of his soul.

We should invite The Spirit of God to search us as found in Psalm 51:10 (KJV), "Create in me a clean heart, O God; and renew a right spirit within me."

Duncan Campbell

In his book, Why Revival Tarries, Leonard Ravenhill states that "The Cinderella of the church today is the prayer meeting. This handmaid of the Lord is unloved and unmoved because she is not dripping with pearls of intellectualism, nor glamorous silks of philosophy, neither is she enchanting with the tiara of psychology. She wears the homespuns of sincerity and humility and so is not afraid to kneel!"

For the Christian, prayer is the direct communication or access to the heart of God as seen in James 5:16 (KJV), "The effectual fervent prayer of a righteous man availeth much."

When it comes to the life of Duncan Campbell and the Hebrides Revival, the Christian needs to give thanks for two women of God. These two women were both disabled and unable to attend church services. One sister was blind and the other sister's body was riddled with arthritis.

However, they were active warriors when it came to prayer and called upon Him to show His glory in a mighty and revealing way. The Scripture verse, Isaiah 44:3 (KJV) that overwhelmed them was, "I will pour water on him that is thirsty and floods upon the dry ground."

As a prelude to Duncan Campbell being involved in this revival, the story is told that he was preaching without success. In fact, in his own words, he described his spiritual leadership in 1942 as "being in a spiritual wilderness and he being in a backslidden condition."

The years progressed for Duncan Campbell and in 1949; he was the minister at the Faith Mission Convention at Hamilton Road. Duncan Campbell was a Presbyterian minister and the church was located in Bangor, Northern Ireland.

However, it was here in this pastorate that he would utilize a motorcycle and go back to the Isle of Skye. This Island was where he once ministered previously. In terms of Christian success God was using him to convert individuals to a saving knowledge of The Lord Jesus Christ.

It was at this point in time that he received the call to go to the Island of Lewis. Initially he resisted the call, but God had other plans and many doors were closed in regards to this ministry and the Island of Skye.

Additionally, despite the commitment that he was scheduled to bring the sermon the following day, Campbell suddenly felt compelled to leave at once.

In tandem, come to find out, the prayer warrior sisters asked that a minister be sent for. The sisters were not given a name, but received a vision of a man standing at a pulpit.

In fact, upon arriving at the Island of Lewis, he was met by an elder of the local church. This particular leader in the church was so confident that Campbell was going to preach at the church, he had already announced to the congregation his arrival without actually receiving confirmation.

Duncan shares that the night of revival came following his delivery of his message. Nothing occurred during or following the sermon, however Duncan says that he and a young deacon were walking down the aisle and the young man implored God to reveal Himself.

The young deacon spoke The Word. The verse he stood on was the same verse the two sisters were given regarding water on the thirsty and floods upon the dry ground.

The floodgates opened and The Holy Spirit descended upon the assembly. The congregation began to weep uncontrollably begging for God's mercy and grace. Some members stood for hours with their hands stretched heavenward while others fell to the floor in true Holy Spirit repentance.

Additionally, it is recorded that at a dance nearby, 100 young people were in attendance. The Holy Spirit descended down up those in the dance hall and they all ran for the church to seek God and beg for His mercy. It is estimated on that night, over 600 people flocked to the church with an additional 400 seeking the Presence of God outside the police station. It is estimated that on that one night, close to 1,500 people were revived by The Holy Spirit of God.

The most important lesson that we can learn from Duncan Campbell and his involvement with the Lewis awakening is the power of prayer. Specifically, two elderly women with debilitating diseases prayed that God would be glorified and that signs and wonders would follow His presence raining down upon.

It is critical to understand the value of waiting upon The Lord and praying. Our prayers should not be selfish and asking for blessings to be showered upon His people and His church. Our prayers should be that the glory of The Lord would be revealed in this world through His church and that people would be brought to a saving knowledge of Jesus Christ and filled with the power of The Holy Spirit.

Please note the importance of Acts the first chapter as well as Acts the second chapter. In Acts the second chapter The Holy Spirit descended down upon those who were in the room, but in Acts

1:14 (KJV) we read, "These all continued with one accord in prayer and supplication, with the women, and Mary mother of Jesus and with his brethren."

The were praying and waiting for revival.

And so, it is important to remember that even the greatest orator, the greatest preacher or the greatest revivalist needs the power of prayer lifting them up to the throne of grace.

In particular, when thinking about the life of Duncan Campbell, it is also encouraging to note that he felt like he was in a backslidden condition. I believe that most of us feel that we have some time or another lived a life of compromise when it comes to our relationship with The Lord. However, God does not cast those individuals away, but like the potter He places the clay upon the potter's wheel as seen in Jeremiah 18:4 KJV which reads, "He made it again another vessel, as seemed good to the potter to make it."

The early life of Duncan Campbell also reveals the possibility that he was probably discouraged. This is a supposition. However, his wife was stricken with an illness and a number of pastoral responsibilities were abdicated because of dissension within the church. These experiences led him to describe this period of time as backsliding and being enveloped in a spiritual wilderness.

It seems that experiencing a spiritual wilderness in each of our lives is part of the cross of Christ.

The wilderness was experienced by Moses, by Noah and by Christ Himself. The wilderness is an experience of temptation, sacrifice and learning of spiritual lessons. The success of the wilderness is finding oneself reduced to God and God alone.

God was preparing His preacher for this moment in time.

Finally, there are many instances in the life of Duncan Campbell where he exhibited sensitivity to God and was led by The Spirit despite other forces leading or requiring him to be elsewhere. One definition of sensitivity can be stated as defined by Merriam-Webster as an "awareness of the needs and emotions of others."

In a spiritual sense, sensitivity could be equated to a closeness of relationship with God. Our sensitivity towards God should be at a point of being aware of His Presence, His direction, His voice, His silence, etc. A sensitivity and a relationship that we can only achieve by meditating on His Word and practicing His Presence through His Holy Spirit.

Katherine Kuhlman

Kathryn Johanna Kuhlman was born in Concordia, Missouri on May 9, 1907. Born of German parents she was one of four children. Her mother was not a loving mother and was harsh and showed little love or affection.

At the age of 14, she was converted while attending an evangelistic meeting held in a small Methodist Church. In addition, what formed the ministry of Kuhlman was the fact that her sister Myrtle had married an itinerant evangelist by the name of Everett B. Parrott.

On one occasion the preacher, Parrott, was unable to stand in the pulpit. Consequently the two sisters preached the message that day. Upon hearing the powerful message delivered by Kathryn, a pastor of that church encouraged Kathryn to step out on her own. Her sister Helen joined her.

The first sermon that she delivered, after receiving this direction, was in Boise, Idaho. Following this premier sermon she then continued to travel within Idaho as well as branching out to Utah and Colorado over the ensuing five years.

It is important to note that at this juncture, in the study of Kuhlman's life, to discuss women teachers and their role in the pulpit. Many denominations refer to I Timothy 2:12 (KJV) in regards to not allowing women to teach. Paul says, "But I suffer not a woman to teach, nor to usurp authority over the man, but to be in silence."

Many biblical scholars will argue that this was the traditional norm for the day in regards to the role of the woman as it related to religious education.

Additionally, if one was to do a word study on this verse they will see that rather than there being two injunctions, a woman not to teach nor usurp authority, there is really only one prohibition. The word nor in the Greek language is *oude*.

In other words, according to this verse by Paul, there is only one limitation for a woman and that limitation is not to usurp her authority over a man (in actuality, this limitation would apply to both men and women because neither genders have authority over the other. Our authority is God and we should be in service to each other).

Therefore, through the Greek word, *oude*, it is one limitation and women should not teach with self-imposed authority over men (https://www.charismanews.com/opinion/45688-does-1-timothy-2-12-really-say-women-can-t-teach-in-church).

Anyway, who can argue with God on whom He chooses to call and use as His vessel in reaching out to others.

In 1933 the sisters relocated to Pueblo, Colorado and there they utilized an abandoned warehouse for their evangelistic meetings as well as eventually traveling to Denver. The building utilized in

Denver was entitled the Kuhlman Revival Tabernacle and The Lord gave them success. Eventually the congregation grew to over 2,000 members.

During this time of ministry she began to realize the importance and power of the broadcast media. There she began a radio show called "Smiling Through" and invited others to utilize airtime. One of those individuals was a minister by the name of Phil Kerr who preached on divine healing. Additionally, another invited evangelist was a minister by the name of Burroughs Waltrip.

Her interaction with Waltrip proved to be a significant turning point in her life.
This minister was very charismatic and easy on the eyes. Consequently, a relationship developed between Kuhlman and Waltrip and they married in 1938. Unfortunately, Waltrip was married and had two children at the beginning of their relationship.

A potential learning from this event in Kuhlman's life is that, because of her sin, she would no longer prove useful to God. However, it is not for us as believers to be the judge of such actions. We as recipients of the fullness of God's grace are instructed to be gracious to others as well.

This does not excuse sin nor does sin in the church need to be overlooked.

There needs to be discipline.

In Galatians 6:1 (KJV) we read, "Brethren, if a man be overtaken in a fault, ye which are spiritual, restore such an one in the spirit of meekness; considering thyself, lest thou also be tempted." Also, in I Corinthians 5:5 (KJV), "To deliver such an one unto Satan for the destruction of the flesh, that the spirit may be saved in the day of the Lord Jesus."

As a result of this sin many left the church. Subsequently, following their marriage, she and Waltrip moved to Mason City where they went into full-fledged ministry utilizing the radio. Unfortunately, because of Waltrip's demands and income not being what it should be, the board resigned in total and left Waltrip alone to deal with the negative financial situation. Unfortunately, the radio chapel went into bankruptcy with Waltrip's last sermon being in 1939 in the month of May.

The following years proved to be very difficult as they went back to being itinerant evangelists. Additionally, because of their marital history, many local churches would not allow them to utilize the pulpit and in 1947 the couple divorced

However, please note that in the continuing biography of Kathryn Kuhlman she is restored to fellowship and empowered by the Holy Spirit to continue on the work The Lord had appointed her to do.

A year prior to the divorce, in 1946, Catherine Coleman was invited to speak in Pennsylvania in the City of Franklin. It was there that she was well received and decided to stay in the area. She also began utilizing the radio pulpit again in Oil City, Pennsylvania. Eventually, this radio ministry, blessed by God, became popular and was broadcast in the City of Pittsburgh as well.

Her ministry focused in on the healing power of God. Through this ministry, many miracles were attributed to the healing power of God through this radio ministry. One such miracle, in 1947, included a woman who was cured of a tumor while listening to Kuhlman preach. Some Sundays later a man was also healed while Kuhlman was teaching about The Holy Spirit.
Her contemporaries at this time included William Brown, Oral Roberts and A.A. Allen. It proved to be a God glorifying time of miracles.

One other conflict arose in Kuhlman's life, due to her preaching the fullness of The Holy Spirit to other denominations and their believers who could meet at the foot of the cross. One denomination was the Catholic Church and reaching out to this faith gained her much criticism.

Katherine Kuhlman was very engaging and charismatic herself and generally, auditoriums were filled to the maximum when she stood behind the pulpit.

In 1968 she was ordained by the Evangelical Church Alliance. Hundreds of healings have been attributed to her being a vessel of God and her teaching about the power of The Holy Spirit

One particular demonstration that often characterized her ministry was when God appeared in these meetings people would be "slain in the spirit."

However, to Kuhlman 's credit she never took credit for any of these healings but always pointed to the Great Physician, Jesus, and that He is their Healer.

The life and ministry of Katherine Kuhlman is an inspirational story of a woman called by God to be His servant, preach the good news and be a Spirit filled vessel to bring about miraculous healings in His name.

Her life also testifies to the fact that God's grace and the power of the blood of Jesus Christ is greater than our shortcomings and our acts of disobedience. We should never listen to the evil one when it comes to our actions. Our justification to stand in the Presence of God is only attained by the finished work of Christ, not on our own merits.

Finally, Katherine Kuhlman was a woman. Being a woman did not minimize her role in The Kingdom. Our standing is in Christ and may the words of Galatians 3:28 (KJV) sink deep into our being and break down the walls of division. That verse reads, "There is neither Jew nor Greek, there is neither bond nor free, there is neither male nor female: for ye are all one in Christ Jesus."

Conclusions:

In Acts 19:1-7 (KJV), we read that Paul came to Ephesus and found certain disciples there. It is possible, that after a little fellowship and interaction with these disciples, Paul realized that they had not received the baptism of The Holy Spirit. Therefore, in these verses, we read, ""And it came to pass, that, while Apollos was at Corinth, Paul having passed through the upper coasts came to Ephesus: and finding certain disciples, He said unto them, Have ye received the Holy Ghost since ye believed? And they said unto him, We have not so much as heard whether there be any Holy Ghost. And he said unto them, Unto what then were ye baptized? And they said, Unto John's baptism. Then said Paul, John verily baptized with the baptism of repentance, saying unto the people, that they should believe on him which should come after him, that is, on Christ Jesus. When they heard this, they were baptized in the name of the Lord Jesus. And when Paul had laid his hands upon them, the Holy Ghost came on them; and they spake with tongues, and prophesied. And all the men were about twelve."

In these verses, it is important to note, that it is obvious that they had not received the baptism of The Holy Spirit. Furthermore, the 12 disciples that Paul came in contact with had not even heard about The Holy Spirit. Paul then asked what baptism they received and the 12 disciples responded that they had received the baptism of John. Of course, Paul said that is all well and good, but that was the baptism of repentance.

In other words, Paul is saying that there is so much more, so abundantly more that God has in store for you through the baptism of The Holy Ghost.

And so these 12 individuals had their own personal Pentecost as they were baptized in the name of The Lord Jesus and The Holy Ghost came upon them and they all began to speak in tongues and also they prophesied.

For these 12 disciples in Ephesus there was more. Their salvation was not fully complete for The Holy Spirit had not come upon them and in them. They had received The Jesus who died on the cross for the deliverance of their sins, but they did not experience the ascension of Jesus and His gifts to mankind. This promise is seen in Ephesians 4:8 (KJV), "Wherefore he saith, when he ascended up on high, he led captivity captive, and gave gifts unto men."

Dear reader, "Have ye received the Holy Ghost since ye believed?"

This short study has endeavored to show the generational workings of God The Holy Spirit.

We have embraced The Holy Spirit as we once again have been reminded that The Holy Spirit is a member of The Trinity. In addition, we understand that He has a personality and that he is always moving and always moving forward.

In the Old Testament, he came upon men and women for specific reasons and purposes during particular times so that God would be glorified and His people would once again be reminded of His great love, grace and providential care.

In the New Testament we are overwhelmed that a new dispensation occurred. The Holy Spirit came in all of His fullness at Pentecost. He arrived like a mighty rushing wind and when He came He transformed and revolutionized the life of the believer as well as creating an upheaval in the world in which the believer lived.

The Spirit filled Christian becomes a flame that ignites their life as well as setting the world on fire as well. Through the power of The Holy Spirit, the Christian turns a world, that is upside down, right side up.

We then proceeded through the various generations of history and became more keenly aware that our God is a God of history. He writes the history because he is in the history and nothing occurs or happens without His permission or His direction.

He is The Creator, Governor and Preserver of all things. He is in control. Despite the fact that things may appear chaotic, godless or destructive, God is still on the throne. Hallelujah!

And so through these generations and through these historical eras, God always had a man or a woman that he got a hold of and utilized them through the power of His Spirit.

Sometimes, these men and women stood up against false doctrine when the church was going down a path of self-indulgence and destruction. They stood up to the false teachers of religion despite the perils that faced them both mentally and physically. These men and women could not be bought because they were already purchased by the blood of Jesus Christ and were His bond servants.

We also witnessed various Christian movements being born by The Spirit of God. The leaders that God called and empowered were ordinary men and women, but they had a hunger for God. God used this hunger to draw them closer into his heart and to experience His fullness so that they could revolutionize their present-day society as well as bringing spiritual worship back into focus. That focus being for the glory of God, evangelizing the lost into a saving knowledge of Jesus Christ and then transforming those believers through the presence of the power of God The Holy Spirit.

And through this generational study we saw the methodical march of God The Holy Spirit working with His church to "go ye into all the world and preach the gospel."

In particular, during the 20th century, we saw revival after revival of God's church as witnessed through the outpouring of His spirit. In Joel 2:28 (KJV), we read and witnessed this promise, "And it shall come to pass afterward, that I will pour out my spirit upon all flesh; and your sons and your daughters shall prophesy, your old men shall dream dreams, your young men shall see visions."

We have spiritually traveled on a steady march with God The Holy Spirit as we have traveled from Egypt, as seen in the Old Testament, to the upper room in Jerusalem, to Ephesus, to Rome, to England, to America and to Africa. Each of these revived locations testify to an upper room experience as men and women received Holy Ghost fire and lit up their world, evangelized the lost and spread the full gospel of Jesus Christ.

We have endeavored to share that the command, as found in Mark 16:15 (KJV), is still relevant and has not been rescinded. To be reminded, those words are, "And he said unto them, go ye into all the world, and preach the gospel every creature."

In closing, one last story.

Have you heard about a man by the name of George Washington Goethals?

Goethals was an officer in the United States Army and eventually became an instructor at West Point. Outside of being a military officer, Captain Goethals was an engineer and taught at West Point from the years 1885 to 1889.

In 1891 he was promoted to the rank of captain and, because of his engineering experience, was put in charge of building the Shoals Canal on the Tennessee River. His insight and success as an engineer was readily made apparent when along this river he supervised the building of a ingenious lock that, up until this time, had been unprecedented.

His military history also included his supervision of the engineers who volunteered during the Spanish American War.

Subsequently, because he was noticed by upcoming presidential leadership, William Howard Taft, he was eventually appointed by President Theodore Roosevelt to be the head engineer in charge of building the Panama Canal.

The hopes of building a successful canal through the country of Panama was almost doomed from the start. In his leadership role, Goethals faced many tremendous obstacles.

First and foremost, was the project itself. What was required for the building of this canal would be enormous locks that would facilitate the passage of the ships through the canal system.

Additionally, because of it being a massive undertaking, there were many individuals needed to ensure its success. It is estimated that 30,000 employees were hired on to build the Panama Canal. As one can imagine the housing and feeding logistics itself was a massive undertaking, but when you add in diseases such as malaria and yellow fever it certainly added to the complexities of being successful with this project.

Additionally, as with any project or undertaking that could be deemed as noteworthy and with credit being given to people, there were the naysayers. These critics were saying that it was too expensive and couldn't possibly be done. They were very skeptical of the project and in particular highly criticized leadership for undertaking such a project.

In particular, they had Goethals in the cross hairs.

On one occasion, an assistant asked Goethals how he was going to respond to those who were criticizing this project that he was working on and predicting that it would never be completed.

Goethals replied, "In time." "How?" the man persisted. "With the canal," Goethals stated.

On August 15, 1914, the Panama Canal was opened to commercial traffic.

It is not known whether Lt. Colonel George Washington Goethals was a Christian. However, his answer to his assistant in addressing the critics is the same answer that we as Christians can powerfully give to a world that is disbelieving or wishes to discredit us and the church of Jesus Christ.

We can answer "with the canal" or, for us, by being filled with The Spirit of God and with that filling of us as vessels show forth miraculous signs and wonders.

Other Books By the Author

- Mountaintop Boulevard - The Pilgrim's Journey into Bliss
- Don't Quit- Your Best Days Lie Ahead
- A Walk Into Eternity - An Inevitable Expedition of the Human Race
- Kingdom Attitude for Contagious Christian Living (ebook)
- Godpreneur – Tapping the God Principles That Framed The Universe
- 100 Days of Heaven on Earth...Warfare Prayer Guide

Contact Details for the Author:

Email: gmattoki@gmail.com

Facebook ID: www.facebook.com/gbenga.owotoki

Twitter: www.twitter.com/GbengaOwotoki

Instagram: https://www.instagram.com/gbengaowotoki

Made in the USA
Columbia, SC
05 July 2022

62711063R00095